Discipline in the Classroom:
Solving the Teaching Puzzle

Discipline in the Classroom: Solving the Teaching Puzzle c.1

Robert G. Howell, Jr., M.S.
Patricia L. Howell, M.S.

Reston Publishing Company, Inc.
A Prentice-Hall Company
Reston, Virginia

Library of Congress Cataloging in Publication Data
Howell, Robert G
    Discipline in the classroom.

    Includes bibliographies and index.
    1. Classroom management. 2. School discipline.
I. Howell, Patricia L., joint author. II. Title.
LB3013.H675   371.1'02   79-16482
ISBN 0-8359-1344-9

Meryl Goodman Thomas, Production Editor

To Trent and Morgan

Contents

Preface

A basic goal of all teachers is to meet their students' educational needs by imparting a body of knowledge that is deemed useful and necessary by teacher, school board, and school district staffs. This seemingly simple goal is achieved only after an incredible amount of effort on the part of teachers, administrators, ancillary personnel, such as psychologists, counselors, speech therapists, nurses, and secretarial and custodial staffs. Despite long years of training and a burning desire to help children learn, many teachers find themselves facing disciplinary situations each day that interfere with both their teaching and their students' learning. Learning to deal effectively with students' acting out, forgetfulness, carelessness, lack of interest or participation in classroom assignments is generally a long process of trial and error on the teacher's part. Eventually, the teacher learns how to handle most problems. However, the amount of time and effort that goes into this process drains much of the teacher's energy and enthusiasm.

Most teachers feel that they must spend too much of their precious teaching time dealing with disruptive classroom elements. In some classrooms such dealings may reach epidemic proportion and dominate the curriculum. Many teachers, both new and veteran, will at one time or another find themselves in a teaching crisis—a class that is out of control. Knowing what to do when this occurs, or better yet, knowing how to prevent it from occurring is the focus of this book. Many educators seem to feel that correct handling of disciplinary problems results only from years of teaching experience. We, on the other hand, feel that teachers can use this text to structure the educational environment in their classroom to avoid many classroom disciplinary problems and to handle the remaining problems more easily.

The basic orientation of the authors is that discipline and the instructional program cannot be separated. To make this statement, we must specify which definitions of "discipline" we are using. We are not talking of the limited sense of discipline that is "the treatment that corrects or punishes."[1] This, unfortunately, is what many people think of when they hear the word. Rather, we speak of discipline as "the training that develops self-control, character, or orderliness and efficiency,"[2] and we believe that no body of curriculum can be taught without considering these aspects of the students' behavioral makeup. This training combined with a third meaning of discipline, that is, a branch of knowledge or learning, is the heart of the teaching process.

We believe that it is impossible to teach effectively without considering classroom discipline carefully. Good classroom discipline is more than having the students obey you. It is the total process of teaching children to participate voluntarily and fully in your classroom educational activities. Your discipline strategies should do more than squelch inappropriate behavior. They should constantly reinforce the desirable behavior that is basic to the development of the total classroom instructional program. For example:

- Getting all of your students participating willingly in all classroom activities.

- Getting your students to pay attention to your directions—to do what you ask the first time you ask it.

- Getting your students to complete assignments.

- Getting your students to come to class prepared—bringing appropriate or necessary materials, books, etc.

- Getting your students to pay more attention to you and the lessons than to the antics of the classroom clown, to the acting out of disruptive students, to the hottest gossip on campus, or to their own daydreams.

- Getting your students to cooperate with you—to do perhaps unpleasant (or at least un-fun) activities without power struggling and arguing every inch of the way.

Are these concerns of yours? Most likely they are—if you are either presently teaching or student teaching. If you worry about your own effectiveness in handling student behavior and school–related problems, read on. This text will provide you with solutions for some problems and understanding at least of the underlying elements of others, as we help you to become a more effective teacher.

---

[1] Joseph H. Freend and David Guralnik, eds., *Webster's New World Dictionary of the American Language, College Edition* (Cleveland and New York: The World Publishing Company, 1959), p. 416.
[2] Ibid.

This text is a practical guide for all teachers. Although many techniques contained herein may be valuable at the high school level, we have chosen primarily to direct our comments to teachers of elementary and junior high school classes. Here the need for effective discipline programs is the strongest, in the years when patterns of school behavior are being developed and before the biggest benefit of the aging process, maturity, begins to appear and make a real difference in student performance. This text will serve teacher needs whether they are beginners or seasoned veterans, or whether they are working in regular or special education programs. It is aimed at both working professionals and students or practice teachers who have learned how to teach the three R's of reading, writing, and 'rithmetic, but who now need to deal with the three C's of coping with student misbehavior, conquering school anxieties, and constructing vitally necessary positive programs of classroom discipline.

Briefly stated, the goals of this text are twofold.

1. To determine the basis of teacher tensions and anxieties and show how these can be overcome to improve the instructional program.

2. To evaluate the teaching process to determine how the components of school physical environment, classroom interpersonal dynamics, curriculum, student behavior, student-teacher communication and the interpersonal relationships of the teacher to the parents, teachers, and school administrators can affect discipline and be used to improve it.

Acknowledgments

The authors would like to thank the many persons who assisted in the preparation of this manuscript. We are deeply indebted to Dr. Martin Baren for his technical assistance with the figures of Chapters 1 and 2, as well as his support and critical advice throughout all phases of the preparation of this manuscript.

We wish to thank Linda Lavine, Cathy Thrasher, and Donna Wallis for graciously allowing us to share their teaching ideas in Chapter 5.

We gratefully thank Robert Joy for his assistance in improving the parent-teacher conference section of Chapter 8 and for allowing us to present his Parent-Teacher Conference Sheet.

We offer our sincere thanks to Eugene Kreyche, whose comments and years of experience as director of personnel, greatly assisted us in making Chapter 9 reflective of trends, needs, and concerns in that area.

We are sincerely indebted for the cooperation of students and employees of the Orange Unified School District. Our particular thanks go to: Shirley Goodman—for her good ideas and tremendous help in obtaining photographs for the manuscript; Dave Bastin and Jim Gibson—for their photographic expertise; Principal Larry Heim, Anita Haupt and her students—for allowing their class to be rearranged so many times; and Dr. Lynn Cook and the students and staff of Handy Elementary School—for sharing their model program of conflict management in Chapter 4.

We are also grateful for Jack McCullough's suggestions and criticisms during the earliest stages of our formulating this manuscript.

We wish to acknowledge the artistic abilities of Elisa LoBue, who assisted in turning our thoughts into pictures in the puzzles located at the beginning of each chapter.

To Jan Fukai goes our most sincere thanks for the hours she spent in deciphering and typing our scribbles.

And finally, thank you, babysitters: Rosemary Altepeter, Ben and Marianne Cohan. Without your help we never could have finished it.

Introduction

What will this book do for you? Will this text simply be another shelf clutterer, good in theory, but weak in practice? We certainly hope not. We've designed a book that we feel will acquaint teachers with the skills and techniques that are needed to deal successfully with disciplinary problems and thus will be able to reduce teacher anxiety while improving learning. We recognize that many different tools, techniques and levels of communication, will be needed to teach the diverse groups seen by all types of teachers. However, in every successful teaching situation, a universal characteristic of strong classroom discipline can be found. Learning is facilitated and student behavior may be changed to become desirable when the teacher is in control. We feel the teacher must practice preventive teaching—an aware, knowledge-based type of teaching that will allow the teacher to be in command of all instructional/disciplinary situations regardless of his or her own anxiety levels. Preventive teaching, like preventive medicine, tries to stop undesired things from happening. As disease hampers the physical development of the individual, so does disruptive student behavior and poorly used facilities or personnel hamper the educational development of the individual. It makes as little sense to wait until the disease strikes before innoculating as it does to wait until you have a student outbreak of disruptive behavior before trying to decide what should be done. Anticipative action is the vaccine that teachers must use to prevent problems in their classrooms. The practice of such actions will be defined in greater detail and in terms of actual teacher behavior in structuring sound instructional programs in the ensuing chapters.

The importance of anticipative action will appear repeatedly as we discuss how a teacher's management of variables affecting discipline in the classroom can lessen teaching anxieties while improving the total instructional program. To teach effectively, teachers cannot and should not allow themselves to drift through instructional activities at the mercy of their surroundings and circumstances. For this reason, we have devoted a complete chapter to the inspection of the effects of each of the following variables upon the instructional/disciplinary program:

1. School physical environments

2. Classroom interpersonal dynamics

3. Curriculum management

4. Student misbehavior and the motivation of appropriate classroom behavior

5. Student-teacher communication, both verbal and nonverbal

6. Interpersonal relationships between the teacher and parents, fellow teachers, and the school administration and nonteaching staffs.

We hope that our discussions in these areas will make you more aware of the importance of the effects of these variables upon your day-by-day dealings with students and your total teaching style in general. Once these elements are clearly understood and you take the time to assess their effects upon your teaching situation, you will have laid the foundation for a sound disciplinary structure in your classroom. Such assessments and your subsequent anticipative action based upon those assessments are the habit of successful teachers.

Up to this point, we have been sharing our philosophy of what constitutes successful teaching and disciplinary programs. As we have stated in the preface, we do not feel that the two (teaching and discipline) can be separated. Our reasoning for this is that you cannot teach unless you get your students' attention and retain that attention throughout the entire learning activity. Perhaps it would be more correct to say that while you may teach without your students' attention, they will not necessarily learn without it. Your students' attention will be greatly determined by your management of the six educational variables that we listed earlier. As an introduction to this text, a brief definition of each of the aforementioned variables and a description of how they will be dealt with in the following chapters may be helpful to you at this time.

Student behavior or misbehavior does not occur isolated from all that happens around it. It is contingent upon a multitude of factors, not the least being the physical environment—the classroom where the learning is to take place. Educational programs must be designed with a careful consideration of environmental confines and extraneous variables if they are to be successful and avoid disciplinary problems. We will enumerate these variables as well as provide strategies for dealing with the "unchangeables" of classroom settings. Also to be considered will be the importance of teachers' familiarizing themselves with the procedures, personalities, and attitudes of the total school environment.

Classroom interpersonal dynamics is a concept that is overlooked by many teachers when they are setting up educational programs. Although peer group relations are dealt with constantly, few teachers attempt to objectively determine how the various student personalities affect each other and the teacher. For this reason, the discussion of sociograms, their construction and usage, will be included to provide teachers with a valuable tool for both preventing and squelching student misbehavior. Besides considering student personality dynamics, teachers who practice anticipative action should also consider the personality dynamics of all teaching and ancillary personnel before they are hired or assigned to a classroom. However, the necessity of using that personnel correctly to enhance the possibilities of learning and positive student behavior is extremely important and will be discussed.

Student behavior, as we have stated, is an outgrowth of many complex stimuli. Curriculum management, that is the decisions made by teachers and school districts of what to teach and how to teach, is a major determinant of student behavior. Although teachers may be told what to teach and what books to use to teach, they are not powerless to avoid classroom struggles if they take care to prepare lessons that meet student needs and interests. We will discuss how organization, time management, and flexibility in lesson planning can help save a "doomed lesson" and prevent negative student behavior. Another factor that will be considered is the importance of teachers' establishing relevant expectancies for student performance. Expecting too much from students can quickly lead to student disinvolvement and rebellion. Also, students who attempt projects far beyond their capabilities and fail are not likely to willingly take part in future activities. The student response, "No, I am not going to do it!" will be discussed and strategies outlined for dealing with this behavior before and after it occurs.

Once the subject matter of the educational program has been decided upon and lessons planned carefully to meet the needs of the students, the next important principles to consider are those of evaluating student misbehavior and providing motivation for improved behavior. We will discuss individual definitions and tolerances of misbehavior and provide techniques for observing, recognizing and recording such behavior. Such tools as the Premack Principle, contracting and point systems, will be discussed to show their merits in training your students to participate freely and fully in your classroom instructional program.

Teacher-student communication has a great effect upon the success of the total instructional/disciplinary program. Although teachers are generally aware of what they are saying, of the points they are trying to make, they are not always aware of the way they are saying it, or the effects of non-verbal messages upon their students' behavior. For this reason, a chapter will be devoted to a discussion of the modes of classroom communication and their effects upon student behavior. Techniques for improving the quality and clarity of communication will also be discussed.

Dealing with parents and faculty members can also affect the teacher's successful management of student behavior and discipline. Once teachers determine that they need outside help in controlling student behavior, either with an individual or the entire group, they must be very careful in enlisting aid from outside sources such as parents, counselors, administrators, fellow teachers, and staff members. Guidelines for asking for such help will be discussed so that teachers will be able to avoid some common pitfalls. Positive conferences with parents can yield valuable results in the areas of student behavior within the classroom. For this reason, suggestions for establishing good rapport with parents and discussions of the makeup of positive parent-teacher conferences will be included.

A final category to be considered that generally affects the teacher's construction of a successful learning/discipline program is the need for achieving philosophical agreement between teacher, district and site administration policies for handling student discipline problems. All three of these groups want students to learn and behave properly, but may have greatly differing definitions of, or expectations for, proper student behavior. This disparity will be discussed. The subject of teacher rights, especially as they relate to student learning and behavior, will also be discussed.

This text has been designed to provide you with an understanding of the functioning of psychological, sociological, and emotional states present within the teaching situation *in general* and disciplinary situations *in particular*. We believe that lowering teacher anxieties in the classroom will increase the likelihood of teacher success and student learning. For this reason, we have devoted two chapters to teacher tension. The first chapter will discuss teacher anxiety—its sources, incidence, and effects. Techniques for discovering the source of your own classroom-produced anxieties and eliminating the negative effects of such anxieties will be illustrated and further discussed in Chapter 2.

Note to the Reader:

To maximize your utilization of this text, we have included exercises at the end of each chapter entitled "Thinking it Through," which are intended to personalize the information contained therein. Also while you are reading through the chapters, we suggest that you make notes in the margins whenever you feel that a concept or situation relates to you or your classroom. Such notes and exercises will help to move the information out of the theoretical and into the real world of actual teacher-student behavior and problem solving. The more you can become actively involved while reading the chapters, the better you will be able to integrate the techniques of anticipatory action into your own teaching repertoire.

1 Anxiety and the Classroom Teacher

When considering the emotional state of many teachers I see in the classroom, I've often thought that present day teachers also wear the scarlet letter that was worn by Nathaniel Hawthorne's Hester Prynne. The "A" no longer stands for adulteress however—now it stands for *anxiety* and has significance for all who see it and bear it.

Leo J. Schmidt, Ed.D.

Teachers, being people themselves, are subject to all the same anxieties and pressures as the rest of the human race. We are sure you may regard this as a rather obvious statement. However, teachers are often considered only as a professional group and, unfortunately, their humanity is overlooked. This book, if it does nothing else, is meant to talk about people, not just about characteristics of a vocational group. It will consider how people behave. It will recognize their needs and assess how those individual needs may conflict, interact, or promote growth through group workings. We will see how people (who also happen to be teachers) can become more efficient and do their jobs, no matter how complex they are, with less stress and anxiety.

The Complexity of Teaching Anxieties

Anxiety, stress, tension, and pressures are four frequently used terms in our society. Popular magazines and newspapers on the newsstands constantly headline new treatments for stress and anxiety. Equally prolific in discussing stress and its treatments are paperback books in supermarkets and professional journals, texts, and experimental studies in libraries and university bookstores. Everyone is interested in stress and anxiety because everyone suffers from them in varying degrees.

Teachers suffer the effects of anxieties derived from a great variety of sources. Such complex teaching anxieties are often responsible for making your teaching assignments difficult and may leave you with more daily dreads and worries than people working in other professions. Like them, teachers have all of the average personal problems to solve—such as worrying about finances, family illness, or feelings of insecurity due to some major or minor disruption in their personal lives. Added to these universally-felt anxieties, teachers must also deal with anxieties which grow from the characteristics of individual teaching assignments. The needs, problems, and anxieties of the total community daily enter your classrooms in the personages of your students. Problems and personal crises at home greatly affect a child's participation in the school program. Disruptions in the child's performance, in turn, negatively affect the teacher's performance. Such disruption in learning or behavior, which is due to problems generally beyond your control, can cause you to question your own teaching ability and will create an additional source of teacher anxiety.

Teachers are in the difficult position of most middle managers in that they accomplish their goals largely by managing relationships. They rely upon the support, cooperation, and approval of a large number of people, including students, parents, fellow teachers, administrators, ancillary personnel, school board and the general public (if they work in tax-supported public education programs). The fact that these various groups may sometimes have conflicting ideas over what should be done in the classroom can lead to producing further teacher anxiety. How can you

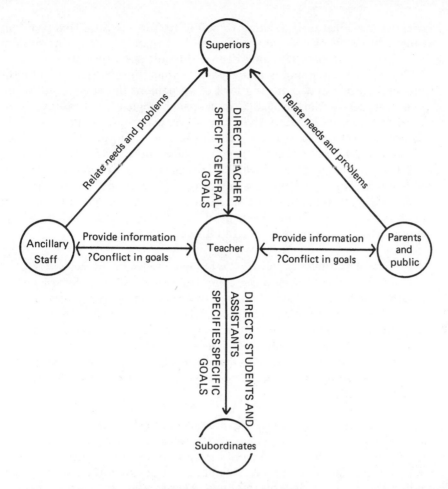

The World of Teacher Anxiety   Figure 1.1

possibly please everyone, teachers ask in frustration. Figure 1.1 depicts the dynamics of this struggle where teachers try to accomplish the demanding "threefold task of middle-management requiring the middle manager to act as subordinate, equal, and superior."[1] Is it any wonder that the rapid shifting in these positions, so necessary to successful teaching, can result in additional classroom anxieties?

Defining Anxiety to Make It a Workable Construct

Lessening the effects of these anxieties upon the classroom educational program is a problem that educators, psychologists, sociologists, and

---

[1]   Hugo E. R. Uyterhoeven, "General managers in the middle," *Stress, Success . . . and Survival* (Harvard Business Review, 1976), p. 70.

physicians are constantly seeking to solve. Before tackling this problem we must first define exactly what we mean by "anxiety." This is a problem in itself because anxiety has long been a difficult term to define.

The problem in defining anxiety is not that there is any lack of definitions, but rather that there is a lack of agreement between a multitude of definitions. As a matter of fact, more psychological studies have been devoted to examining anxiety than any of the other emotional states.[2] As T. R. Sarbin states in an article explaining the "opaque nature of anxiety,"[3] the term did not appear in psychological and psychiatric texts until the 1930's. Although derived from a translation of Freud's *Hemmung, Symptom und Angst,* our present–day usage of anxiety differs from that of Freud's reference. This has been the major problem of defining anxiety throughout the years. It has been used to refer to a wide variety of circumstances and conditions. As stated in Sarbin's article:

> The inkblotlike nature of "anxiety" is further revealed by the multiplicity of referents. Some referents are expressed in terms of overt behavior such as tremor, coughing, stuttering, and twitching; some in terms of complex conduct such as avoidance, defense, and denial of stimulus inputs; some in terms of antecedent events such as aversive stimuli and memory of traumatic events; some in terms of heart rate, GSR, and respiratory rate; and some in terms that have only vague subsistent referents such as apprehensions, emotional states, states of mind, affects, and feelings.[4]

Thus, anxiety is a word that can be used to refer to a wide variety of conditions and effects. It can be both a stimulus and a response. Above all, it can be said to be highly individualistic, with its characteristics dependent both upon the individual experiencing it and the circumstances surrounding it. For example, you might be able to address a large group of people without any signs of anxiety if you are secure in your knowledge of the subject matter, but turn into a fearful, trembling, perspiring mess when you have to speak "off the cuff" on an unfamiliar topic.

Response Modes—The Different Faces of Anxiety

We could all probably accept our anxieties more complacently if these physiological signs and emotional states did not interfere with our lives and work to the extent that they do. Tension headaches, ulcers, and re-

---

[2] Frederick H. Kanfer and Jeanne S. Phillips, *Learning Foundations of Behavior Therapy* (New York: John Wiley & Sons, Inc., 1970), p. 134.
[3] T. R. Sarbin, "Ontology recapitulates philology: The mythic nature of anxiety." *American Psychologist,* Vol. 23 (1968), p. 415.
[4] Ibid.

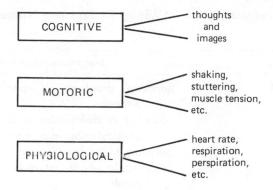

The Response Modes of Anxiety   Figure 1.2

duced feelings of self-worth are just a few of the problems that are associated with anxiety. Such problems can work into a snowballing effect to further reduce teaching effectiveness. The overlap of your feelings and anxiety reactions to one activity with your students can seriously affect the success of your activities for the rest of the day, week, or year if you do not understand or control the negative effects of anxiety in your classroom.

To understand and deal with teaching anxieties, you must first analyze the total circumstances surrounding the moment of stress to determine a "performance-oriented" definition of anxiety that Thomas J. Coates and Carl E. Thoresen call for in their very thorough review of teacher anxiety.[5] Figure 1.2 presents the response modes upon which such an analysis is based. The cognitive, motoric, and physiological modes are the three ways in which anxiety is typically experienced. All three of these modes are interrelated and are part of a complete performance-based definition of anxiety. Coates and Thoresen feel that relating these behaviors or modes to other teacher and student behaviors in specific classroom situations can be used to pinpoint both the sources and consequences of teacher anxiety. Thus, an awareness of how you are feeling, as well as how your actions affect the behavior of others, can help to reduce your anxieties about your students' as well as your own performance.

Determining the Sources of Your Anxiety

What makes you tense as a teacher? This important question has been asked repeatedly in surveys of teacher anxiety. The answer differs with

    [5] Thomas J. Coates and Carl E. Thoresen, "Teacher Anxiety: A Review with Recommendations" (Research and Development Memorandum No. 123, Stanford University, 1974), p. 10.

Table 1.1   Reported Sources of Anxiety for Beginning Teachers

Study	Reported Sources of Anxiety
1. Wey (1951)	handling problems of pupil control and discipline adjusting to deficiencies in school equipment, physical conditions, materials adjusting to the teaching assignment adapting to needs, interests, and abilities of pupils motivating pupil interest and response
2. Travers (1953)	discipline will pupils like the teacher?
3. Gabriel (1957)	class control evaluation by inspectors
4. Anderson (1960)	ability to bring about learning ability to maintain classroom control contractual stipulations orientation to the school system faculty relations
5. Ahlering (1963)	grading papers arguing over test answers restlessness of students handling discipline problems attending college and doing student teaching at the same time introducing new ideas to stimulate discussion cheating by students
6. Dropkin & Taylor (1963)	discipline relations with parents methods of evaluating teaching planning materials and resources classroom routines

(continued)

the type of teacher asked, the passage of time (if the differing answers are due to changes in attitude rather than changes in the focus of survey questions), and the individual teacher (as we have stated earlier, anxiety is very much an individual matter). Naturally, student or beginning teachers are going to have different anxieties than those of experienced teachers. Some of the differences between these two groups are shown in

Study	Reported Sources of Anxiety
7. Thompson (1963)	what will critic teacher expect of me? what will these pupils be like? what should I do if my material has been covered and there is extra time? will I be required to turn in my lesson plans and who will evaluate them? do I really know my subject matter? will pupils like me and respond to my guidance? will I be able to maintain desired standards of behavior?
8. Erickson & Ruud (1967)	knowing enough to teach the units how will I be evaluated? what will my supervising teacher be like?
9. York (1968)	common clusters of problems fell into the following categories: discipline academic organization individual differences planning
10. Sorenson & Halpert (1968)	disagreements about what and how to teach personality conflicts with supervising teachers difficult relations with students
11. Yee (1968)	negative interactions between student teacher, supervising teacher, and collect supervisor
12. Fuller (1969)	concerns with self how adequate am I? where do I stand? (is this my class or the supervising teacher's class?)
13. Valencia (1971)	method of providing feedback about teaching performance
14. Fuller & Manning (1973)	viewing teaching performance on videotape microteaching practice in area teacher is not concerned about

Tables 1.1 and 1.2. The tables, reprinted from the Coates and Thoresen study, show the differing responses of the two groups to surveys conducted from 1939–1973.[6]

---

[6] Ibid., pp. 5–6, 8–9.

Table 1.2   Reported Sources of Anxiety for Experienced Teachers

Study	Reported Sources of Anxiety
1. National Education Association (1939)	class interruptions: bulletins, announcements, errands, special events adapting class program to individual differences in ability, interest, need adapting promotion standards to meet a "no-failure" ideal without neglecting "minimum essentials" expected by the school or without endangering future school adjustment and progress of pupils clerical activities—mimeographing class materials, work sheets, transcribing records, test results for central files, etc. total number of pupils assigned size of individual class
2. National Education Association (1951)	number or type of pupils inadequacy of school facilities (e.g., restrooms) extracurricular responsibilities clerical and administrative work instructional planning
3. National Education Association (1967)	insufficient time for rest and preparation in school day large class size insufficient clerical help inadequate salary inadequate fringe benefits
4. Susskind et al. (1969)	incompatible relationships with supervisor: his petty demands, inability to communicate with him, his anger when things are not done his way assignment of paraprofessional duties: standing on guard in yard, standing on guard in lunchroom discipline problems: children chewing gum, getting out of seats and walking around room, coming to school without homework, talking and making noise while the teacher is trying to teach, making constant comments, running out of classroom

(continued)

Study	Reported Sources of Anxiety
5. Olander & Farrell (1970)	finding time for individual and remedial work working without benefit of a daily preparation period obtaining funds for the purchase of extra classroom aides finding time for creative teaching planning lessons, grading papers, completing report cards
6. Fuller (1969) Parsons & Fuller (1972)	concerns with pupils: ability to understand pupils' capacities, to specify objectives for them, to assess their gain, to determine one's contribution to pupils' difficulties and gains
7. Thoresen et al. (1973)	growing line at pencil sharpener student at teacher's desk student says "I don't have a pencil" as teacher begins quiz students not paying attention as teacher gives directions while teacher is assigning seats, a boy says "I don't want to sit with the girls" students get noisy as teacher talks to superintendent in room student says "Teacher, what am I supposed to do?" as you finish giving directions two students fighting over a basketball student becomes belligerent when teacher corrects him one boy says, "I won't do it" when teacher gives students instructions principal says, "We don't have enough money" when teacher makes suggestions that would help him to do a better job of teaching

A quick look at Table 1.1 shows us that the beginning teacher's anxieties are focused on the unknown:

1. Will I be able to teach children adequately?

2. Will I be able to maintain discipline?

3. Will I have sufficient knowledge of subject matter?

4. Will I be able to relate to students, parents, other teachers and supervisors?

These questions are answered as the school year passes. When the answers are positive, the beginning teacher's school-based anxieties are light and probably create no further problems. If, however, the answers are negative, second–stage anxieties begin to grow. At this point, anxieties must be dealt with constructively so that they do not jeopardize the total instructional program as well as the teacher's feelings of his or her own self-worth.

The more experienced teachers have a different struggle. They develop a different set of questions based on anxieties that developed as the result of the known, real-life experiences in the teaching world:

1. Will I have time to accomplish my goals?

2. Will I be able to effectively minimize the interruptions of student disruptive behaviors?

3. Am I producing? Am I doing a good job? Do I really make an identifiable difference in my students' growth and learning?

These worries do not dissolve with time. The answers to these questions are constantly changing as your circumstances and students' needs and behaviors change. This self-assessment discloses the source of most teachers' deepest anxiety—the fear of being an unsuccessful or ineffective teacher.

The Magnitude of the Fear of Failure in Teaching

Perhaps the reason teachers fear being unsuccessful is that there are so many spectators in the classroom when they do fail. If it is human nature to look quickly around to see who has seen us when we trip or stumble, then it is natural that you would be highly sensitive or embarrassed about your academic or professional stumbles when you are on stage with about 30 pairs of eyes watching. More important, your stumbles or failures may also result in your students not learning things that are important to their development. Thus, your failures will become their failures and such failures are recognized by your colleagues as the students pass along to the next teacher's class. They are also noted by despairing parents and a critical society in general as the students move into the world seemingly unskilled and unprepared to meet the demands of life.

Educational failures cannot be equitably compared with those of industry. In industry, when products have defects or do not sell, the loss in profits can in part be made up by selling defective or damaged goods as seconds. There is little market for the young adult who has not learned to read or has not acquired necessary skills for the labor market. This fear of not being able to prepare your students adequately to perform well in society is not inconsequential. So much is dependent upon the teacher's performance that you have good cause to worry about how well you are doing.

This does not say, however, that you are totally responsible for all of your students' failures and learning deficiencies. When discussing students being obstacles to their own learning, teachers are constantly asking the following questions:

1. If the students do not try to learn, what can we do?

2. How can we educate those who see us and other school personnel as the ultimate authority figures and use all their efforts to thwart us rather than learn from us?

3. Can we force people to learn if they don't care to?

These concerns are shared by teachers in all districts with students of all races, abilities, and socioeconomic groups. You will all be forced to deal with such students. The best approach to dealing with anxieties about your ineffectiveness with such problem students is *not* to write them off as lost causes and forget about them. That does both you and them a disservice. If you care to expend the energy and the time necessary to analyze those students' behavior in terms of the total educational climate and restructure key elements, you can motivate them to participate voluntarily in classroom activities. This book will serve as a guide for breaking down the problems encountered in the classroom into behavioral units. The key is preparing yourself, your classroom, and positive classroom activities in such a way that prevents many problems before they occur and allows you to handle the remaining problems more effectively. Once done, this preparation will alleviate many of your anxieties about teaching and discipline-related problems.

The Need for Being in Control of Anxiety

Although we have been speaking of your anxieties' dark nature, the side that makes you sick, ineffective, and fearful, we cannot overlook the fact that anxieties can work to your benefit. Although working in an anxious state is not as pleasant as working in a relaxed state, your work need not always be detrimentally affected by anxiety. Sometimes your fear of failure may force you to overprepare lessons, developing so many energetic activities and stimulating supplementary materials that your lucky students feel they have just entered some kind of academic Disneyland. Also, that extra push from adrenalin coursing through your veins may help you through some difficult situations with acting-out or disruptive students. When this works, your anxiety seems to supply you with the extra strength needed to say or do the right thing to break up a fight or avoid a major and futile confrontation with a student. However, anxiety cannot always be counted on to help you. At its worst, it can cripple your instructional program.

Major Instructional Cripplers—Teacher Paralysis and Overreacting

As we have stated repeatedly throughout this chapter, people who teach may be beseiged at times by anxieties. Whether these tensions pass or seriously affect your functioning as a teacher, is greatly dependent upon your individual tolerance of pressures. Although some people thrive under pressure, others bog down.

Consider this common occurrence in a classroom: An activity, which you have successfully conducted previously, begins to fall apart because one problem student chooses to wander around the class disturbing the work of others. If you have had success in dealing with this child in the past, the odds would be that you could handle the problem again. If, however, you have failed in getting him back to work in the past, you are likely to start worrying about getting him to work again. As you are preoccupied with this student, others lose interest in the activity and you really become anxious. Not sure what do to, you raise your voice, calling for order, using a shotgun approach to deal with unwanted behavior. Most of the students go back to work but some never do resume their tasks. Now, instead of teaching the major group, you are angrily dealing with the subgroup of nonworkers. In terms of teaching, you are instructionally immobile.

This teaching paralysis can occur whenever anxiety or the effects of anxiety chronically begin to impair classroom activities. If your worries make you avoid activities, students and subject matter, you have teacher paralysis. Strategies for avoiding such paralysis will be presented in the remaining chapters.

The second serious effect of out-of-control teacher anxiety is overreacting. This occurs when you are fatigued, anxious, and your patience is about gone. A student's insolent remark may have gone overlooked earlier in the semester or even in the day. But now this disrespectful remark takes on the weight of that one last straw that broke the camel's back. You explode and say things that you would not have said under better circumstances.

The biggest problem with overreacting is that it generally produces second generation anxiety—anxiety in your students. When the teacher overreacts in the classroom, a subtle but prevailing atmosphere of pressure builds and the students become more anxious. This is unfortunate because children already live in a highly stressful world. In his article on children's stress, Dr. Martin Baren states that "the one group in our society under the most repeated and long-lasting stress is our children. Their problems start at birth (or before in many cases) and grow as the children do. Each phase of a child's life represents change and adaptation both for the child and his parent."[7] Children's reactions to their own stress is of much importance to the classroom teacher. As the childhood pressures increase with the passage through school and into adolescence, their behavior may become more nonproductive. Their anxieties can make them angry and likely to overreact, shy and withdrawn, or more clinging to the mores of their peer group (which may be very much in opposition to yours). It is important that your students' stress be relieved, not compounded by second generation anxieties. Such anxiety transference greatly hampers both your students' educational growth and your teaching success. Thus, the effects of anxiety can spoil school for both you and your students.

Throughout this chapter, we have presented a bleak picture of the effects of anxieties on teaching and teachers. The picture need not be completely gloomy, however, because you can control your anxieties and, in many cases, erase them. This is done by learning the three C's of *coping* with student misbehavior, *conquering* school anxieties, and *constructing* vitally necessary positive programs of classroom discipline. A discussion of how this is to be accomplished will begin in the next chapter.

---

[7] Martin Baren, M.D., "Stress: Our Kids' Greatest Health Hazard," *Coronet,* 15, No. 2, p. 107.

1

1. List at least five feelings or thoughts that may be signals of your own possible anxieties in the classroom.

2

2. How do these physiological or psychological signs (modalities) affect your teaching style?

3

3. When you are feeling stress . . .
   a. are your students aware that you are tense?

   b. do they ignore your tension?

   c. do they behave the same as when you are relaxed?

   d. do you notice more behavior problems in the classroom?

4

4. Using the following chart, record your feelings of stress at the same time each day to see which times or days during the week are most stressful for you.

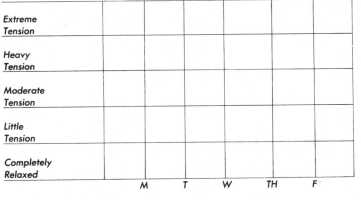

Days of the Week

Ahlering, Inez, "Reactions by Student Teacher," *Clearinghouse,* 37, (February, 1963), pp. 337–340.

Anderson, Harold S., "Prospective Teachers Have Fears," *Clearinghouse,* 34 (February, 1960), pp. 337–341.

Baren, Martin, "Stress: Our Kids' Greatest Health Hazard," *Coronet,* 15, No. 2 (February, 1977), pp. 107–113.

Coates, Thomas J. and Carl E. Thoresen, "Teacher Anxiety: A Review with Recommendations." Research and Development Memorandum No. 123, Stanford University Center for Research and Development in Teaching, 1974.

Dropkin, Stanley and Marvin Taylor, "Perceived Problems of Beginning Teachers and Related Factors," *Journal of Teacher Education,* 14, No. 4 (December, 1963), pp. 384–390.

Erickson, Joan Kleinert and Josephine Barton Ruud, "Concerns of Home Economics Students Preceding Their Student Teaching Experiences," *Journal of Home Economics,* 59, No. 9 (November, 1967), pp. 732–734.

Freud, Sigmund, *Hemmung, Symtom und Angst.* Leipsig, Vienna and Zurich: Internationaler Psychoanalytischer Verlag, 1926.

Fuller, Frances F., "Concerns of Teachers: A Developmental Conceptualization," *American Educational Research Journal,* 6, No. 2, (March, 1969), pp. 207–226.

Fuller, Frances F. and Brad A. Manning, "Self-Confrontation Reviewed: A Conceptualization for Video Playback in Teacher Education," *Review of Educational Research,* 43, 1973, pp. 469–528.

Gabriel, J., *An Analysis of the Emotional Problems of Teachers in the Classroom. London: Angus and Robertson, Ltd.,* 1957.

Jersild, Arthur T., *When Teachers Face Themselves.* New York: Teachers College Press, 1955.

Jersild, Arthur T., Eve Allina Lazar, and Adele M. Brodkin, *The Meaning of Psychotherapy in the Teacher's Life and Work.* New York: Columbia University Press, 1962.

National Education Association, "The Teacher Looks at Teacher Load," *Research Bulletin,* 17, No. 5 (1939).

National Education Association, "Teaching Load in 1950." *Research Bulletin,* 29, No. 1 (April, 1951), pp. 3–50.

National Education Association, "Teachers' Problems," *Research Bulletin,* 45 (1967), pp. 116–117.

National Education Association, "The American Public School Teacher, 1965–1966," *Research Reports,* R-4 (1967), pp. 3–57.

Olander, Herbert T. and Mary E. Farrell, "Professional Problems of Elementary Teachers," *Journal of Teacher Education,* 21, No. 2 (Summer, 1970), pp. 276–280.

Parsons, Jane S. and Frances F. Fuller, "Concerns of Teachers: Reliability, Bipolarity, and Relationship to Teaching Experience." Paper presented at the meeting of the American Educational Research Association, Chicago, April 1972.

Petrusich, M.M., "Some Relationships Between Anxiety and the Classroom Behavior of Student Teachers." Doctoral dissertation, University of Washington (Ann Arbor, Michigan: University Microfilms, No. 66-12038), 1966.

Runkel, Phillip J. and Dora E. Damrin, "Effects of Training and Anxiety Upon Teachers' Preferences for Information About Students," *Journal of Educational Psychology, 52, No. 5 (October, 1961), pp. 254-261.*

Sarbin, Theodore R., "Ontology Recapitulates Philology: The Mythic Nature of Anxiety," *American Psychologist,* 23 (June, 1968), pp. 411–418.

Sellinger, S., "An Investigation of the Effects of Organizational Climate and Teacher Anxiety on Test Anxiety of Elementary School Students." Doctoral dissertation, New York University (Ann Arbor, Michigan: University Microfilms, No. 72-11494), 1972.

Sorenson, Garth and Ruth Halpert, "Stress in Student Teaching," *California Journal of Educational Research,* 19 (January, 1968), pp. 28–33.

Susskind, D.J., C.M. Franks, and R. Lonoff, "Desensitization Program with Third- and Fourth-Grade Teachers: A New Application and a Controlled Study." Paper presented at the meeting of the Association for the Advancement of Behavior Therapy, Washington, D.C., September, 1969.

Thompson, Michael L., "Identifying Anxieties Experienced By Student Teachers," *Journal of Teacher Education,* 14, No. 4 (December, 1963), pp. 435–439.

Thoresen, Carl E., T. Alper, J.W. Hannum, J. Barrick, and R.N. Jacks, "Effects of Systematic Desensitization and Behavior Training With Elementary Teachers." Unpublished paper, Stanford University, 1973.

Travers, R.M.W., W. Rabinowitz, and E. Nemovicher, "The Anxieties of a Group of Student Teachers" in *Exploratory Studies in Teacher Personality,* eds. R.M.W. Travers, W. Rabinowitz and M.H. Page.

New York: City College, Division of Teacher Education, Office of Research and Evaluation, 1953.

Valencia, S.M., "Anxiety Cued Verbal Responses in Student Teachers," in *Exploratory Studies in Teacher Personality,* eds., R.M.W. Travers, W. Rabinowitz, and M.H. Page. New York: City College, Division of Teacher Education, Office of Research and Evaluation, 1953.

Wey, Herbert W., "Difficulties of Beginning Teachers," *School Review,* 59, No. 1 (January, 1951), pp. 32–57.

Yee, Albert H., "Interpersonal Relationships in the Student-Teaching Triad," *Journal of Teacher Education,* 19, No. 1 (Spring, 1968), pp. 95–112.

York, L.J.N., "Relationships Between Problems of Beginning Elementary Teachers, Their Personal Characteristics and Their Preferences for Inservice Education." Doctoral dissertation, Indiana University (Ann Arbor, Michigan: University Microfilms, No. 68-4761), 1968.

2 Conquering Classroom Anxieties

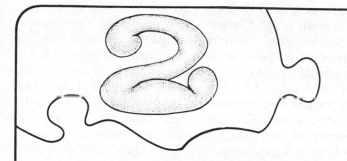

. . . to teach we must know the people we teach and the obstacles to learning (and teaching) that exist. To know the people we teach we must recognize that anxiety plays, or may be playing, an important role in their lives and in our own.

Arthur T. Jersild
When Teachers Face Themselves

In our previous discussion of anxiety, we generally stayed within the psychological framework from which the term grew. However, limiting our discussions to the psychological realm would not be too beneficial to teachers. After all, how many classroom teachers care that anxiety is experienced in three modalities or that it is opaque by nature? Teachers do care about the fact that anxiety, if left unchecked, can make their teaching assignments unpleasant and themselves sick. Thus, they generally want to control their classroom anxieties as much as possible. Discovering which situation or person in your classroom makes you anxious is not always easy. Your feelings or experiences of anxiety may build gradually and you may feel the worst when the source of anxiety is no longer present.

Too often discussions of anxiety dwell upon emotional states and overlook the more prevalent physiological signs that can plague us. The down-to-earth feelings of anxiety that teachers experience vary and include such complaints as stiff necks, sore arms, headaches, tight back muscles, upset stomachs, and general feelings of tenseness and depression, to name a few. Often a professional may seek counseling due to feelings of depression. When such feelings are explored, however, a combination of complaints such as lack of sleep, tense and irritable feelings, and headaches, all due to anxiety, have led to this generalized feeling of depression. Thus, it is easy to worry about the wrong things—to spend time trying to solve one problem when in fact another is causing you difficulty in the classroom.

By now, you may be finding this discussion of anxiety a little depressing in itself. How, you may be already asking, do we deal with something as puzzling as anxiety? We have enumerated many sources and signs of anxiety in Chapter 1. Now the time has come to discuss how to eliminate, or at least control, these sources and manifestations.

Avoiding Self-Created Anxieties—A Key to Reducing Classroom Pressures

The normal stage fright or new-on-the-job jitters that many teachers experience will hopefully diminish as teaching success and experience grows. There are situations, however, that can undermine the security of teachers with years of experience and success. No one is free of anxieties when tried and true methods no longer seem to be effective with certain problem students. As an example, one teacher who had taught eight years and had been highly successful ran into the following problem. Setting the scene briefly, this person loved teaching and was considered to be one of the most effective teachers on the staff by peers, students, and administrators alike. Then Dave entered her program mid-year. Reading Dave's cumulative records alone was enough to turn many a seasoned veteran's hair white. Dealing with him was even worse. Although this teacher had had success with difficult students before, she could not seem to bring him around, try as she would. Dave sought to gain everyone's attention, but he was not interested in doing so by excelling in or even participating in any classroom activities. Instead, whenever she would have an exciting lesson underway,with most of the class having a good time learning, he would manage to cause a fight, call someone a name, or verbally interfere with the group's acitivity to the extent that no one could enjoy or benefit from the activities. He did not respond to her attempts to stop this unwanted disturbance. Instead, he got so bad that she became convinced he was out "to get her." When he was absent, which was frequent, the class went like clockwork. When he returned, the chaos started once more. Although she felt as though she was a complete failure, she turned to the school administration for help. She wanted Dave out—permanently.

Although Dave's behavior was the major source of difficulty in this struggle, the teacher's own mental set also contributed greatly to the problem. Her tension grew as much from her own self-fulfilling prophecy as it did from his behavior. In such a prophecy, the actual results of a situation are greatly dependent upon one's own expectations. Dr. Robert Merton, the sociologist who developed the concept of the self-fulfilling prophecy (SFP), stated in the film "Productivity and the Self-Fulfilling Prophecy: The Pygmalion Effect"[1] that the SFP starts with a false belief about something. When a person or group acts upon that belief it becomes a true reality. In the Dave vs. Teacher case, the false belief was that Dave was singlemindedly trying to ruin the teacher's lessons. Her self-fulfilling prophecy was based upon his previous school history, and his early lack of response to her combined with his continuing disruptive behavior made all her attempts to solve this problem unsuccessful. Her believing he was going to be impossible before he even entered the classroom may have been partially responsible for the resultant behavior. When such a situation occurs both student and teacher may need objective assistance from outside the classroom to diminish the effects of the self-fulfilling prophecy.

Another researcher, Dr. Robert Rosenthal, a social psychologist, feels that the power of expectation can significantly affect the behavior of others. To prove the validity of this Pygmalion effect, he conducted the well-known study in which each teacher in an elementary school was told that 20% of his or her class were "intellectual bloomers and would make remarkable gains *on their own* during the next eight months."[2] In reality, these "bloomers" had been chosen at random and differed from their classmates only in the minds of their teachers. When tested at the end of

---

[1] "Productivity and the Self-Fulfilling Prophecy: The Pygmalion Effect," Copyright 1974, Ziff-Davis Publishing Co., Distributed by CRM Films, McGraw-Hill, Inc.
[2] Ibid.

the year, this group was four points higher in total IQ than the rest of the class. In other words, the children behaved according to the teacher's expectations.

How the SFP works is not the major consideration here (which is good because no one is sure why it works the way it does). The important thing is that it does exist and may have either positive or negative effects upon your dealings with children in your classroom. As pointed out in the film, the process does not work by magic and is much more complicated than the popular view of the power of positive thinking. It is a social–psychological process that Rosenthal studied in over 30 experiments before developing his four-factor theory of the ways by which positive and negative expectations are conveyed and the Pygmalion effect is established. Expectations are conveyed by:

1. *the total climate,* which includes all nonverbal messages such as body language and eye contact
2. *feedback,* in which the amount of response that is given depends upon how much is expected
3. *input,* where the nature and amount of information given for task completion is dependent upon the level of expected performance, and
4. *output,* where the amount of encouragement for future efforts is also dependent upon whether expectations are positive or negative.

Thus, the teacher's mental set is instrumental in the students' accomplishing their goals. Since teachers are also middle-managers (see Chapter 1), the value of this concept that has been found in industry can also be seen in the classroom. Rensis Likert has stated:

> "If a high level of performance is to be achieved it appears to be necessary for a supervisor to have high performance goals and a contagious enthusiasm as to the importance of these goals."[3]

The key to the importance of this contagious enthusiasm lies in effects of both positive and negative expectations of your students' capabilities. If your expectations are high, you are much more likely to get good results and if your expectations are low their performance is more likely to be poor.

Avoiding creating negative or disruptive student performance with your expectations is crucial to your overall teaching success. Negative Pygmalion effects can, in part, be eliminated by not putting as much emphasis on what you read in cumulative records or hear through the grapevine as you do on what you actually see take place in your classroom. If you have been told that you have "a tough class" this year or that a cer-

---

[3] Ibid.

tain student is the original Johnny Tornado and you allow yourself to develop a belief that this is true before enough evidence has been presented, you are well on your way to making a self-fulfilling prophecy. Once you have encountered difficulties with a student or a tough class, then you must take care not to become too hardened against them. Before allowing yourself to be drawn into an "it's either them or me" power struggle, seek some outside help. Perhaps the parent, school psychologist, counselor, or another teacher may be able to suggest some positive interventions before you become too locked into a no-win situation for you and your students. Thus, your anxiety will be relieved and you will be able to more fully understand your students' behavior. You also can restructure the classroom climate more successfully when you keep in mind the inevitability of the influence of your expectations upon both your treatment of students and their subsequent performance.

Additional Strategies for Dealing with Anxiety

The Age-Old Physiological Responses: Fight vs. Flight

As you are teaching and struggling with instructional and/or disciplinary problems and your anxieties are building, your body will probably react in time-old ways. Humans and animals have reacted to stressful situations in a predictable fashion for centuries, perhaps millions of years. This physiological response, the fight–flight response, is considered by Herbert Benson to have evolved from man's fight for survival, and it has been the source of much study and discussion. Benson's work, *The Relaxation Response,* illustrates such responses in the animal world as "frightened cat standing with arched back and hair on end, ready to run or fight; an enraged dog with dilated pupils, snarling at its adversary; an African gazelle running from a predator."[4]

In the academic world we also will find teachers who are choosing between fighting or fleeing from the sources of their anxieties. When faced with a student challenging your authority in the classroom, you must decide what is the best way to deal with this problem. You have the option of handling it or ignoring it. One method of handling it might be by verbally arguing with the student (a fight); while another might be avoiding a confrontation and allowing the student to get away with this disruptive behavior, hoping it would not be repeated (a flight). The results of fights or flights can be both positive and negative in terms of changes in the classroom environment. In either case, when faced with conflict situations that require us to adjust our behaviors in such ways, the involuntary response involved will result in increases in "blood pressure, heart rate, rate

---

[4] Herbert Benson, M.D., with Miriam Z. Klipper, *The Relaxation Response* (New York: Avon Books, 1976), p. 24.

of breathing, blood flow to the muscles and metabolism preparing us for conflict or escape."[5] Such responses fall into the physiological modality of anxiety that was discussed in the previous chapter. If such responses go unchecked and these increases in metabolic rate continue, overstress may occur which can lead to such serious health problems as chronically high blood pressure, heart attacks and ulcers.

The Third Option for Humans—A Defense Against Overstress

The problem-solving capacity of humans can make this decision-making process more positive in terms of desirable classroom results—a lowering of both teacher and student anxieties. As Manuel J. Smith points out in his book, *When I Say No, I Feel Guilty,* the "verbal communication and problem-solving ability is the key survival difference between humans and those species who have either died out, face extinction, or worse, have been domesticated."[6] This third option, of communicating with others and working out problems assertively instead of fighting or running away, is part of an evolutionary inheritance.[7] Our verbal capacity for problem solving is our best approach to coping with what bothers us—all of those sources of our anxieties.

Since controlling tension is a goal of major importance in teaching, improving your problem-solving verbal capacities during times of stress is a crucial determiner of classroom success while avoiding the phenomenon of teacher extinction. Teacher inconsistency is a leading cause of troublesome or stressful situations in the classroom. The probability of student misbehavior increases if teacher expectations and disciplinary tactics vary from student to student and situation to situation. Due to the obvious correlation between student misbehavior and teacher anxiety, consistency in teaching can be seen as the key to dealing with both anxiety and disciplinary problems. The term *consistent* must become the description of the total educational climate, most specifically in the areas of (1) student control, (2) teacher-student communication, and (3) problem solving in general.

Consistency and Student Control. In a booklet prepared for the teacher orientation program of the Woodward Parkway Elementary School in Farmingdale, New York, the concept of teacher sincerity (i.e., consistency) is discussed in the following way:

> Sincerity—Nothing will disrupt a room so quickly and easily as insincerity on the part of the teacher. Children have a keen sense of fairness and often become aware of attempts to camouflage or to deceive be-

---

[5]   Ibid.
[6]   Manuel J. Smith, Ph.D., *When I Say No, I Feel Guilty: How to Cope—Using the Skills of Systematic Assertive Therapy* (New York: Bantam Books, 1975), p. 6.
[7]   Ibid.

fore the teacher gets started. The teacher in turn needs to develop sincerity on the part of the children. When children subscribe to a rule and are continuously allowed to break it, they are learning insincerity. Sincerity can be developed by following through continuously on every rule or standard which is set up.[8]

This discussion restates the importance of consistent adherence to standards of behavior in the classroom. Consider the following illustration of the importance of consistency in student control: one teacher really felt he had met his match in the classroom—a ten-year-old student who was a very strong classroom peer group leader. Not only did she constantly defy his wishes, but she also would disrupt activities and lead other students into mischief. The teacher had lost ground in several early confrontations with this girl and hesitated to compete with her again for fear his authority would become even more diminished. Her behavior baffled him. One minute she would be an aggressive tomboy keeping everyone in place with her physical prowess, and the next minute she would be a simpering Scarlet O'Hara keeping everyone in place with her "charms." Since he preferred dealing with her Scarlet behavior than fighting with her, he decided to try to placate her as much as possible. He allowed her extra privileges and bent numerous rules in order to maintain peace. This inconsistency, or insincerity, however, only led to more misbehavior among the other students and eventually little was left of his authority in the classroom. The students took his rules lightly and classroom discipline was a shambles.

One way to avoid such situations in the classroom is to make only those rules that are absolutely necessary and to enforce them consistently and fairly. There may be times when circumstances dictate that a certain rule be overlooked for the sake of common benefit. However, this should not become a common practice because of the aforementioned possible consequences upon your students' behavior and the total disciplinary climate of the classroom. The teacher in the previous example would have been better off if he had not been so inconsistent in his treatment of his students. In a more structured environment, he would have been better able to change that one student's inappropriate behavior. Instead, his choice of reinforcing either of her manipulative behaviors only led to further problems and more tension. Thus, anxiety can be avoided if you adhere closely to the following principle: if a rule is important enough to classroom functioning to make in the first place, then it is important enough to enforce consistently.

Consistency and Student-Teacher Communication. Consistent thinking and actions can lead to both a positive, well-run classroom and a successful teaching style. Knowing where you are going, by way of pre-

---

[8]   John L. Grindle and M. Genevieve Douglass, *Starting the Year Right* (Dansville, New York: *Instructor,* August 1978), p. 3.

liminary planning and awareness of your own teaching style is the first step. Assessing your students' needs and abilities and designing all elements of the classroom to be consistent with their needs and your general educational goals is the next step. Consistency is indispensable in all of the details of teaching, from your mode of giving directions to seating arrangements or methods of evaluating student performance. Avoiding changing horses in mid-stream is a must in teaching. When you are consistent, you are more likely to be secure in your abilities and the resultant stability in your classroom will greatly lower your anxiety as well as that of your students. Even well-behaved students will become unmanageable if they are trying to find their proper places in a chronically ambivalent classroom. Adherence to educational goals and classroom standards allows your students to know not only what to expect from you but also what you expect from them. This two-way communication is an essential characteristic of a successful teaching and disciplinary program.

Consistency and Problem Solving. The feedback that results from two-way communication is instrumental in improving your problem-solving capacity. If students are clearly aware of the classroom rules and the consequences of breaking rules, they are much more likely to behave appropriately than if they do not know what is expected of them. They need to learn that for every action there is a reaction. Their teacher's reaction definitely tells them what is expected of them. Your students' response to the rules will show *you* how well your educational contingencies are helping you to manage your classroom. If inappropriate behavior continues to flourish, you must decide what is leading to these student disruptions. This is much easier to do if you have an established pattern of teaching behavior. The teacher that changes seating arrangements weekly or classroom rules daily cannot be sure what is the cause of new or recurring problems. The input or feedback you receive from analyzing the results of your consistent strategies will allow you to make changes in the structure based on facts rather than guesses or intuition which may be faulty. The process of such analysis will be discussed in much greater detail in Chapter 6. For now it is sufficient to say that teaching consistently will help you to alleviate many of your feelings of nervousness and insecurity by improving your control of and communication with your students.

Avoiding Anxieties by Preventing Problems

At this point, we are about to conclude our discussion of teaching anxieties. We have tried throughout the first two chapters to accomplish our first goal of showing how anxieties can be overcome to improve your instructional program. It is not the intent of the authors to imply that teachers are nervous wrecks. It is our intent to show they are as human as all other professionals and are subject to the same pressures as those ex-

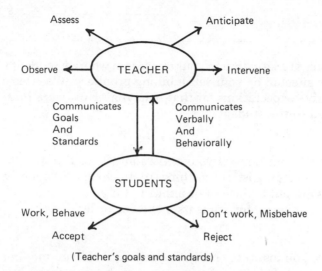

Assess   Anticipate

Observe ◄—— TEACHER ——► Intervene

Communicates   Communicates
Goals   Verbally
And   And
Standards   Behaviorally

STUDENTS

Work, Behave   Don't work, Misbehave

Accept   Reject

(Teacher's goals and standards)

The Practice of Anticipative Action: *The Continuous Motion of Classroom Nuclei*   Figure 2.1

perienced by presidents of companies or any managers of large groups of people. We have used a purely educational model for showing how anxieties can be greatly eliminated in the classroom. For those of you interested in more psychological approaches, further reading into Wolpe's "Process of Systematic Desensitization of Anxieties" might also be beneficial. Also of value would be study of techniques of sensory relaxation such as are outlined in differing ways by Herbert Benson and Bernard Gunther. And those interested in a medical model would find Hans Selye's *The Stress of Life* illuminating.

It is now time to take up our major task of evaluating the teaching process to determine how a wide variety of elements can affect discipline and be manipulated to improve it. Our main goal is to teach teachers how to avoid problems in the classroom. We feel that this will be best accomplished through the practice of anticipative action. Anticipative action is based upon all of the elements that we touched upon in our discussion of consistency. Through anticipative action, the teacher uses feedback from all elements of classroom proceedings to solve instructional/disciplinary problems. The guesswork is taken out of this process by continuous assessment and straightforward communication. Both teachers and students work and communicate together in such a system, each aware of where they are heading and what paths they must take to get there. Teachers are able to prevent problems by anticipating trouble spots and by using the information gained from being aware of the total educational environment to construct a positive program of instructional and disciplinary management. This process is pictorially presented in Figure 2.1.

1 1. Think of a situation in your classroom where a student's behavior was possibly affected by your self-fulfilling prophecy. Was this due to positive or negative expectations for that behavior? How were these expectations conveyed to the student?

2 2. List the constants of your classroom (those things or procedures that do not change). List those things that change frequently. Beside each thing listed, put a plus (+) or minus (−) if you feel that they positively or negatively affect your students' behavior or learning.

3 3. Once you institute change in your class, do you monitor the effects of the change? Do the changes you make generally live up to your expectations?

Benson, M.D., Herbert with Miriam Z. Klipper, *The Relaxation Response.* New York: Avon Books, 1976.

Grindle, John L., and M. Genevieve Douglass, *Starting the Year Right.* Dansville, New York: *Instructor,* August, 1978, p. 3.

Gunther, Bernard, *Sense Relaxation.* New York: Collier Books, 1968.

Jersild, Arthur T., *When Teachers Face Themselves.* New York: Teachers College Press, 1955, p. 26.

Selye, M.D., Hans, *The Stress of Life,* revised edition. New York: McGraw-Hill, 1976.

Smith, Ph.D., Manuel J., *When I Say No, I Feel Guilty: How to Cope—Using the Skills of Systematic Assertive Therapy.* New York: Bantam Books, 1975.

Wolpe, M.D., Joseph, *The Practice of Behavior Therapy.* New York: Pergamon Press, 1969.

3 The School Environment

We never educate directly, but indirectly by means of the environment. Whether we permit chance environments to do the work, or whether we design environments for the purpose makes a great difference.

John Dewey

As we have said previously, student behavior and learning does not occur in a vacuum and cannot be isolated from all that exists around it. Behavior and misbehavior is contingent upon a multitude of factors, not the least being the physical environment where the learning is to take place. The classroom, where the majority of learning activities occur, is only one part of the school's physical environment that concerns the teacher. The location of that classroom in the total school setting, as well as the total school staff's attitudes toward the usage of that classroom, are equally important. For this reason, educational programs must be carefully designed with a consideration of environmental confines and extraneous variables if they are to be successful and avoid built-in disciplinary problems. The following pages will enumerate these confines and variables and then go on to provide some strategies for dealing with "unchangeables" of the classroom setting. Since the environment and work within that environment are influenced by the personalities and attitudes of other members of the total school population, we will also consider the importance of you, as teachers, familiarizing yourselves with school procedures, personalities, and attitudes. We will discuss positive ways of dealing with these psychological parameters.

Analyzing the Classroom's Physical Environment

Before working on any project, a craftsperson generally is acquainted with his or her working space and familiar with the tools and materials needed to complete the project. As basic procedure, teachers are generally careful to assess what materials their students need to complete their assignments. However, not all teachers take into consideration how aspects of the physical environment may interfere with learning and contribute to student misbehavior and resultant disciplinary problems. The ability to analyze all aspects of that setting, knowing which elements of the working or learning space are assets or deficits, is an important step in a teacher's being prepared to combat misbehavior. The wise teacher considers environmental details and tries to improve upon flaws long before any students enter the classroom. Such preparation is important because it can alleviate disciplinary problems before they arise. In this case, the old adage "the best offense is a good defense" is decidedly true. Taking time to consider even the smallest details of classroom size, shape, and composition before setting up activities will be well rewarded once the students arrive upon the scene.

A number of physical variables may affect the classroom instructional/disciplinary program. Each classroom will have its own distinct composition and in a sense "personality" that will greatly influence the success or failure of the educational activities that occur there. Although teaching situations vary greatly, almost all classrooms should be analyzed to determine the effects of the following ten areas before making any long-range plans that are not easily changed:

1. size and possible usage of the work space

2. shape of work space

3. seating arrangement

4. furniture arrangement

5. windows and lighting

6. carpeting

7. heating and air conditioning

8. usage of chalkboards and bulletin boards

9. storage space

10. classroom cleanliness

Your treatment of these variables may differ according to the characteristics of your particular teaching assignment. If you share working space with others in a team teaching situation or move from one class to another several times during a day, week, semester, or year, you will naturally have additional factors to consider. But for the sake of simplification at this point, let's consider each of these variables as though you are solely responsible for the usage of a single classroom.

Structuring the Environment to Avoid Designing Classrooms for Failure

---

Size vs. Possible Usage of Classroom Space

The size of the classroom and the way it is to be used are two very important variables to consider when you first are assigned to your classroom. Unless you teach in a specially designed classroom, such as those found generally at the secondary level, that are used for cooking, science, industrial arts, or physical education, your classroom may be very similar to all others along the school hallway. It is probably of the size deemed appropriate by the school district building planners and the architect for usage by the average number of students per class in your area at the time the school was built. The fact that the school population may have increased greatly since that time may mean that your room will be very crowded with little space for anything other than desks and bodies. This would restrict the type of activities that you can try effectively in the classroom.

Another determiner of classroom usage is the type of subject matter that will be taught there. A self-contained elementary classroom in which all subject areas must be taught may naturally be used differently than a class in a more departmentalized setting. Art projects and dramatic activities may require much more space than seat activities such as reading and individualized paperwork. Your creative impulses, special abilities, and interests may also be affected by the size of the classroom and the number of students to be educated there. A limited amount of space will mean that your students will be brought much closer together, possibly opening the way for horseplay, whispering, and other interruptions in the classroom activities. Unless you decide to restrict movement and have your students do all work in their seats, you will need to consider space usage very carefully when planning activities. Deciding to have your 30-plus students reenact Napoleon's defeat at Waterloo will take much more space and create much more confusion than reading about it or having groups of students depict it in murals. This is not to say that such activities should be avoided, but that they should be carefully structured and provisions made for potential problems before turning your students loose in an already overcrowded room. Your great idea for making learning more "fun and more real" can be made even greater and more successful by thinking through possible strategies for avoiding chaos before plunging into activities.

As school populations grow or change, frequently site administrators are forced to make some very "creative" room assignments. Teachers of smaller groups of students, such as special education classes with restricted enrollments, may find themselves in some unusual places because, as the theory goes, they have fewer students and thus need less space. If you find yourself teaching in an old unused nurse's office, teacher's lounge, storage room or a corner of a huge auditorium you must use your space as the confines dictate. If there is no other place for you to teach, the one consolation that you may draw from getting the worst classroom in the school is freedom to do things within that space because the administrator takes pity on you.

Developing an energetic, imaginative, educational program despite the surroundings can only increase your worth in the eyes of your evaluating administrator and help your students to grow to like their peculiar classroom. Perhaps they will behave even better than they would in a conventional classroom doing more conventional activities.

Classroom Shape and Seating and Furniture Arrangements

Although most classrooms are square or rectangular, the actual dimensions of those shapes will greatly influence the way students' seats and necessary furniture may be arranged. Since seating arrangements can both affect learning and help control student behavior, this is an important consideration. The choice between individual desks or student tables (if that choice is open to you), as well as arranging those seats, may be as dependent upon the amount and the shape of space available in your classroom as the content of the subject matter that you are to teach.

When making appropriate decisions about seating arrangements, you have to decide what is the best way for you to reach the students you are teaching. In order to attain maximum learning and avoid potential disciplinary problems, you must assess your own teaching style and the exigencies of the subject in terms of the effects of the hard facts—the actual dimensions of the room and the availability and arrangements of furnishings.

The proximity of the students to the teacher and each other is the first problem to be analyzed when arranging furnishings. Deciding how far you can spread out the desks without interfering with the students' being able to both hear and see is important. The conventional rank and file arrangement of long rows of desks (see Figure 3.1) is not always the most effective arrangement that can be made. Although it is unlikely that this

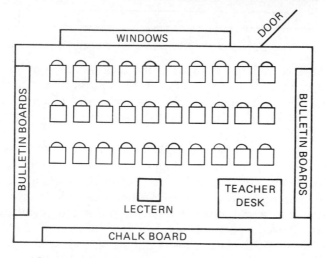

Conventional Rank and File Desk Arrangement   Figure 3.1

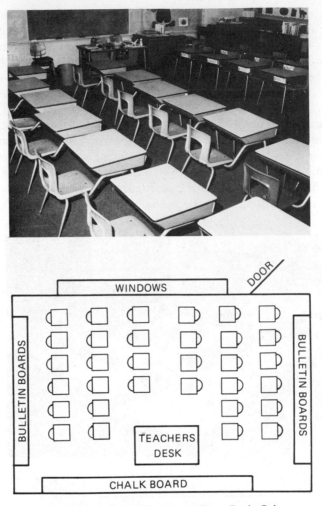

Figure 3.2   Two Halves of the Classroom Face Each Other

arrangement is considered a favorite of educators, it is by far the most prevalent seen in schools. More often than not, desks are arranged this way originally by custodians for the sake of easier cleaning, and many teachers leave them that way without considering how variations might improve the instructional setting.

If, as a teacher, you speak softly or believe the students will need face-to-face communication, you might want to experiment with the following arrangement (see Figure 3.2) in which the student desks are divided into two groups which face each other. This allows groups of eight to ten students to work together without too much furniture moving. Also, you are allowed easier access to the students by being able to move down the middle of the class. This could aid in instruction as well as in discipline. Your physical presence nearby can often squelch student mis-

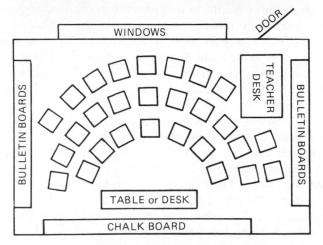

Amphitheatre Desk Arrangement   Figure 3.3

behavior before it is able to get out of hand. Two problems, however, may arise from such an arrangement. First, since each student is facing half of the class, there is more opportunity for the antics of one student to disrupt class activities. Second, the walls at the students' backs are wasted in terms of educational value. They cannot be easily used as instructional aids because one half of the class always has its back to a wall and has to turn around to see it. Such problems are not insurmountable, however, and you may find that the advantages of such an arrangement outweigh the disadvantages.

Another variation in seating that can be used effectively with smaller groups of students (20 or under) is seen in Figure 3.3. This amphitheater arrangement has a number of advantages. One, the students are brought closer to the teacher with maximum allowances for seeing and hearing. There are no heads or bodies interfering with the students' view of the teacher or the front of the classroom. This also enables the teacher to see the students more clearly, making furtive movements, daydreaming, and inappropriate actions and conversations much more obvious. Two, the students are seated farther apart than in conventional settings, thus cutting down on such disciplinary problems as pushing, poking, whispering, and otherwise tampering with other students' belongings and persons. Three, the teacher is able to move much more quickly from one student to another because he or she is not impeded by long rows of desks and can assist students with their work, answer questions and quash rebellions much more easily. Four, the student's total focus is on the teacher rather than on the back of some other student's head, as in the previous arrangements. The students are not seated in a group and as individuals, they are not quite as likely to band together against the teacher. The fifth and final advantage is that the arrangement is more informal and may help inspire a more relaxed atmosphere in the classroom.

This atmosphere of informality may, however, lead to some problems. First, since there is no obvious pattern, as in the rank and file arrangement, students can easily move their desks from the original placement without being very noticeable. If you are not aware of this, you may suddenly find that your audience has gradually inched its way into a corner or away from you. The results of this migration are increased misbehavior and decreased learning. Another possible fault of this arrangement is that it does not look very neat and has no straight rows. From an administrative or custodial point of view, this may be considered both unconventionally unattractive and hard to clean. If the quality of the learning activities is high, the administrator will probably tend to overlook these flaws. Such is not the case of the custodian, however, and it may be necessary to push the desks back into rows each afternoon and rearrange them in the amphitheater in the mornings to avoid open conflict and hostility. One alternative is using this arrangement only when the students are involved in desk work that would benefit from immediate supervision. This arrangement, also called a horseshoe arrangement by Frederick Jones, allows the teacher to move continuously and quickly, helping students who have questions and praising those who are doing well.[1] On a limited basis, this arrangement can be used with even large groups of students as long as the assignment to be worked on is broken down into steps.

In some classrooms where group work is essential or additional work space is needed, possibly student tables are more appropriate than individual desks. Once again, the advantages and disadvantages of such table usage must be weighed and the arrangement carefully considered before actual teaching begins. Tables allow for increased student work space as long as too many students are not forced to sit at each table. Ideally, having the students sit on one side of the table facing forward as in Figure 3.4(a) allows both for more space and ease in lecturing or referring to

---

[1] "Teachers & Teaching," *Education Summary,* August 15, 1978, p. 7.

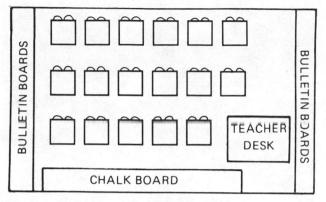

(a)

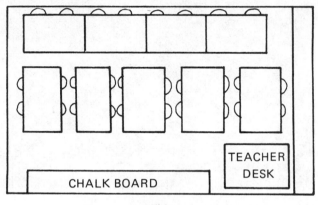

(b)

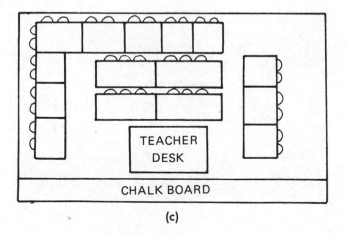

(c)

Variations on Seating Students in Groups—Diagrams   Figure 3.4

(a)

(b)

(c)

Figure 3.4
(Continued)

46

Variations on Seating Students in Groups—
Actual Classroom Situations

charts or chalkboard. If, due to overcrowding, the students must face each other at tables, it may be necessary to consider improved seating arrangements when demonstrations or audio visual aids are being used. Possible variations would be seen in Figures 3.4(b) or 3.4(c). It is far better for you to spend the time and energy moving furniture, even if for one class period, than to lose precious classroom time dealing with students complaining that they cannot see or making seating changes once the 40 students have arrived. Pulling students back down to earth after they have enthusiastically, noisily and chaotically moved desks, chairs, and belongings may be much more effort than you bargained for in the beginning. This is a prime example of cutting off your nose to spite your face. Unless you have excellent control over your students, don't try it.

Seating students around a table in a group, rather than as individuals, may help promote group unity as well as teach them to work together to achieve group goals. To prevent inappropriate behavior from receiving support from the group, making the teacher's job even more difficult, care must be taken to see that the group is working to achieve goals that the teacher believes appropriate. Strategies for achieving such unity and agreement will be discussed in the next chapter.

Combining individual desks and tables may well allow a maximum of flexibility in a teaching situation. Having tables available for group activities may help both to enrich the total educational program and to control student behavior. One combination of individual desks and tables that exemplifies such enrichment and control has been described by Frank Hewett in his book, *The Emotionally Disturbed Child in the Classroom.* In this "engineered classroom" (see furnishings in Figure 3.5) the students receive reading, written language and arithmetic assignments in the mastery center, which is adjacent to the blackboard and represents a traditional classroom arrangement of individualized seating. The two "offices" are provided for students who need further seclusion, either to complete their assignments or to decrease the possibility of their disrupting the total group at work. The tables in the exploratory area are used for science, art, and communication activities. In the order center are activities "emphasizing active participation, direction following and task completion."[2] In these areas, high-interest individual or group activities can occur without disrupting the work of students in the mastery center. As well as providing an area for specialized learning activities, such areas can be used to reward students who have completed assignments and have not been disruptive. Students who must remain in the mastery area while their peers are having fun playing learning games in the back will not be as likely to continue misbehaving in the future. Although this classroom is designed to be used by nine emotionally disturbed students, staffed with an aide and is ideal in terms of both size and furnishings, its basic ideas can be adapted to a variety of surroundings and circumstances. One large

---

[2]   Frank M. Hewett, *The Emotionally Disturbed Child in the Classroom* (Boston: Allyn and Bacon, Inc., 1974), p. 245.

■   MASTERY CENTER

  EXPLORATORY CENTER

▨   ORDER CENTER

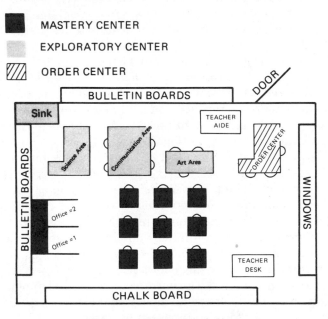

Figure 3.5   Furnishings of an Engineered Classroom

table in the corner of a classroom (Figure 3.6) could be sufficient for an exploratory order center. All that is needed is a space where students can participate in activities away from the area where individualized assignments are given. Many teachers have achieved greater flexibility in their classrooms' atmosphere by providing an informal area in the class where

Exploratory Order Center in the Corner of a Conventional Classroom   Figure 3.6

students can go whenever the teacher deems appropriate. Whether this area consists of a single rocking chair, a bean bag chair or is lavishly furnished will depend upon individual resources and needs.

Minor Variables that Can Cause Major Problems

A teacher who wishes to be well ahead of the game will try to minimize environmental distractions within the classroom. The same windows that let in warm morning sunlight and cool afternoon breezes can become a nuisance if students are constantly gazing out of them rather than attending to class discussions and assignments. Eye-catching bulletin boards, while brightening the classroom, may attract or hold the student's attention more than the teacher's lectures or class discussions. Arranging the desks so the students are not facing the windows or highly distracting bulletin boards may help to minimize these distractions. This will only be possible, however, if chalkboards and other necessary educational aids can still be used to good advantage.

Besides being classroom decorations and instructional aids, bulletin boards can be used to positively change the behavior of the students. If student misbehavior has become a problem, a bulletin board directed toward improving behavior in a prominent place can be a constant reminder of classroom rules. Star charts and check sheets showing appropriate and inappropriate student behavior could also be posted as additional motivators of appropriate behavior.

Noise in a classroom may both interfere with learning and lead to increased misbehavior as students try to talk louder than each other or over background noise and clatter. Classrooms with carpeting are much quieter than those without because the noise of activities is in part absorbed and the vicious cycle of noise making is reduced. Unfortunately, you have no control over getting your room carpeted. If you believe the general noise level of your class is too high and find yourself shouting directions over the hubbub throughout the day, you may need to assess your activities to see if student movement and noise can be reduced during problem activities.

Student comfort may also affect the success of learning activities. Students that are too warm may be too lethargic to participate fully in class activities. Obviously, you may not be able to improve upon your classroom's physical climate if the weather is extremely warm and air conditioning not available. During a heat wave, however, high interest materials, lessons, and activities will be much more successful and appreciated than routine or uninteresting assignments. Thus, although the physical climate remains the same, the learning climate can help compensate for unpleasant conditions. Since an over-heated room may have the same effects of decreased student production and learning, care should be taken to keep the classroom's temperature during the winter comfortable, but conducive to learning.

Generally, classrooms have sufficient lighting for the students to see to do their work. Sometimes, however, too much light can be as big a problem as too little. If, at certain times of the day, classroom windows let in too much sunlight making students uncomfortable or preventing showing a movie, you should try to correct this situation. If traditional window coverings are not available, you may be able to use student work or artistic projects to help block the sun. Care must be taken, however, to comply with school rules concerning window coverings. Check to be sure that the coverings are not a fire hazard and that they do not detract from the school's total appearance.

The availability of storage space within your classroom may affect the overall organization of your educational program. A lack of storage space may mean that certain items must be stored outside the classroom. Many teachers' homes have closets filled with papers and teaching units. Suddenly needing a supplementary ditto that is stored in your garage at home can be a frustrating problem. Keeping materials and supplies (Figure 3.7) neatly organized within the classroom will help activities run more smoothly. Some student misbehavior can be avoided if you are not forced to stop an activity to rummage through papers or books for a needed item.

Reassessing the Classroom Structure and the Need for Change

Once you have assessed the physical characteristics of the classroom and have designed an educational environment that you feel will best fit the needs of your students, instruction is ready to begin. Up until this point,

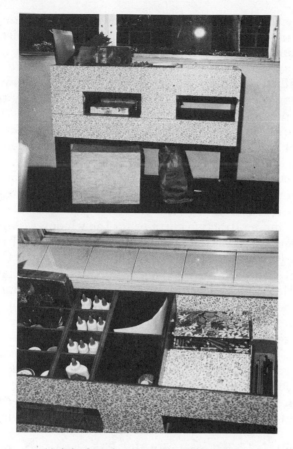

Mobile Supply Unit with All Supplies
Neatly Organized and Easily Accessible During Activities

Figure 3.7

you have been working toward achieving the ideal. Once the students arrive, you are immediately pushed into the real world. In order to sustain a successful teaching and disciplinary environment, you must constantly reassess the structure as the students work and move within it. At this point, you must be as objective as possible and willing to make changes within the structure in order to insure maximum teaching success. The environment will be shaped as much by the students' attitudes and actions as the teacher's. The ability to decide what changes are necessary before your major educational objectives can be achieved will be a prime determining factor in teaching success. A teacher's stubborn clinging to opening day plans and preferences despite their negative effects on student behavior may result in an unsuccessful educational program. Your willingness to change, to adapt the learning climate to the needs of the learners, is fundamental to your success as a teacher.

An illustration of this point is a decision made by one teacher to show an interesting and thought-provoking movie to a group of extremely difficult junior high school students in a private school setting. These students had been thrown out of a number of public school districts because their inappropriate behavior could not be tolerated. As a group, they hated school and said they were not interested in participating in learning activities at all. To combat this, the teacher decided to show a movie that he believed to be fascinating the first day of school to try to catch their interest and perhaps lead them into a discussion. Before this could be done, however, several problems had to be solved. There was no projector at this school and the windows were covered with homemade curtains that in no way darkened the room sufficiently to show a movie.

Since he sincerely believed this movie to be crucial to beginning communication with his students, he decided to rent a projector from a rental company. After much deliberation he also decided to purchase some heavier, more attractive curtains for the windows. This was done at his own expense because the school had limited financial resources and there was no way to be reimbursed before school began. Unfortunately, several unforeseen problems developed and spoiled his plans. First, the film was brittle from overuse and broke every few feet, taking double the amount of time for showing. An even bigger problem, however, arose from the newly purchased curtains. The teacher was unaware of the fact that the dusty, sagging, garish curtains he had taken down were made for the classroom by the girl friend of the class' peer group leader. The class members were proud of the old curtains and hated the new ones the teacher had purchased. Trying to avoid open rebellion, the teacher promised to return the old curtains (luckily he had not disposed of them) but explained that the new ones might be used later to darken the room for movies.

As a student learning activity this film was pretty much a failure. More time was spent discussing the curtains than the film. However, as a teacher learning experience, the activity was a tremendous success. He learned not to expect too much from a single activity. His students would not be won over by a single film. He also learned that despite considerable effort on his part to make everything run smoothly and to structure the environment for success, the advent of students upon the scene with their diverse attitudes and needs is the major factor in determining what will or will not be successful. His willingness to remove the new curtains showed he did not want to spoil his chances for possibly establishing a positive relationship with his students. In this case, stubbornly keeping curtains the students resented would only have resulted in further hostility. The students' reaction to the change in their classroom showed that these "turned off" students were really interested in their classroom's appearance. From this point on, the class was included in decisions on both decoration and curriculum. In part, they decided what was important to learn in "their room." The students' recognition of his interest in them, as well as their own participation in designing learning activities, were at least in part responsible for his later success with these students.

Emphasis of the concept of "our room" is a valuable tool in helping students control their own behavior. If your students feel that you care about their feelings and you allow them a say in room decoration, curricular choice when appropriate, and the selection of classroom behavioral rules, your struggles with inappropriate behavior will be far less frequent than if you autocratically set down all of the rules yourself. Students are far more likely to follow "their rules" than they are to follow "your rules." Teachers often complain that their students do not respect other people's property or rights. Before expecting this behavior from your students, you should be willing to demonstrate your concern over their property. Being careful not to throw away your students' important "stuff" may be a first step in this direction. Often, this may mean distinguishing between garbage and barely salvageable property. Saving student work in folders can demonstrate to students that you care about the work they have done. They enjoy looking at the volume of work they have completed during a semester, and they especially enjoy seeing improvement. Students who have experienced difficulty in completing the assignments especially like to have their work saved. Even if none of the students care to show their work to their parents at the end of the term, you have made a spiritual victory. You showed them that you cared enough to keep their work and have returned it to them to do with as they like. Care should be taken, however, to mention that if they do not want to keep the work, they should discard the work in your wastebasket, not all over the school grounds.

Location of the Classroom Within the Total School Setting

The effect of location of the classroom within the total school environment may often be considered when assessing the characteristics of the classroom's physical environment. For example, what is viewed through the classroom windows may have a substantial effect upon the success of teaching activities. A view of a busy intersection, firehouse, police department or athletic fields may interfere with students' attending to activities. The sights, sounds, and smells outside a classroom can be very distracting and have an adverse effect upon students' behavior. If activity outside the classroom is more interesting than activity within, your job may grow increasingly more difficult as the hours and days pass. Assessing the external distractions of a school site can show that the teachers on the staff can be divided into two categories—the luckies and the unluckies.

The luckies are those teachers who have classrooms assigned to them that have a minimum of external distractions. Outside noise, activities and odors have a negligible effect on these teachers' classes. On the other hand, the unluckies have inherited a classroom in which one or more distractions influence the success or failure of classroom activities. The following list of external characteristics and distractions more specifically states the variety of disturbances that affect classroom activity.

Distractions	Possible Solutions
Disturbing Noise Sources	
Busy intersection with constantly squealing brakes, frequent collisions and noisy trucks Airports and flight paths (generally will affect an entire school rather than a single classroom) Noisy industry such as car repair Sirens from passing ambulances, fire and police department vehicles	Keeping windows closed; arranging furniture so that you are least likely to be fighting the external noise while teaching. Discussing with students appropriate behaviors that will be expected during noisy periods
Band and choir rooms Industrial arts classes with noisy machinery	See site administrator and check to see if schedules can be re-arranged, or class moved.
Classrooms whose teachers have difficulty in maintaining control over students	Talk to teacher first to see if he or she is aware of disturbance; offer suggestions and try to be understanding; if no improvement, see site administrator.
Lawn mowers and gardening or maintenance crews	If such work follows a set schedule, possibly organize activities away from the room when the noisy equipment is due in your area.
Disturbing Odors From:	
Cafeterias Cooking classes	Planning interesting activities to take minds off hunger; check with cooking teacher to see if cooking takes place every day. Maybe plan library period if this becomes a problem.
Businesses with pleasant and unpleasant odors (e.g., dairy farms, canneries, factories)	Keep windows and doors closed if possible.
Distracting Sights Of:	
Administrative office Traffic and intersections Business and commercial areas Athletic fields	As mentioned previously, furniture can be arranged so that the students do not face these distractions; windows can be partially covered by student work or art to interfere with a clear view of outside activities.

There are at least two types of successful teaching experiences. In one, you feel that you are doing a good job in educating the students in your classroom. In the other, school personnel such as other teachers, administrators and custodial staff feel that you are doing a good job in educating your students. How you value your own opinions or those of others may really have great bearing on whether your teaching experience is pleasant and successful on both counts. Stubbornly clinging to your own ideas, preferences and procedures in the face of mounting criticism from fellow teachers and staff members could compound problems and lead to poor evaluations of your teaching abilities. The attitudes of the staff toward your teaching practices may greatly determine whether your stay at a particular school is friendly and fruitful.

We have stated in this chapter repeatedly that your manipulation or acknowledgement of crucial environmental characteristics will have a direct bearing on the success of your classroom programs. In particular, your success in dealing with these variables may be determined by the acceptance of your techniques by the administrators, evaluators, and custodians. Whenever your techniques interfere with the routine of the school or ignore accepted rules, written or unwritten, you may be in for trouble. Examples of such interference would be in arranging desks in such a way that custodial cleanups are made difficult, or by covering up windows with student work that looks great on the inside but unsightly on the outside. Such things quickly will come to the attention of the principal or site administrator and may put you in the unfortunate position of having to explain, change, or discontinue such techniques.

Staff confrontations and ill will may be avoided by carefully considering the feelings of others and school policies before adopting strategies for dealing with environmental problems. Avoiding disagreements with custodians may be accomplished by building rapport with the custodians and getting to know their likes and dislikes and trying to solve your problems without causing more problems for them. If, after discussing your problems with the custodian, you are unable to reach an agreement you may wish to confer with your principal to see if he or she can offer any suggestions for resolving such conflict.

Site administrators, as a general rule, like to be consulted prior to staff members making major changes on the campus, especially if such changes may lead to further staff complications. Speaking from an administrative point of view, the fewer problems the better. Thus, if you can solve classroom problems without disturbing others, your efforts will be generally appreciated. An administrative maxim might be "fix what you can, and accept what you can't fix." From a teacher's point of view you may find this stand disheartening, or even maddening. Although we all hope for support from our superiors, such support may not always be practical or even possible. If you find yourself in a classroom which you feel has a major flaw that interferes with your providing a high quality educational program, communicate your concern to your administrator. If it is not possible to improve upon the situation, perhaps your complaint, if registered positively, will at least partly provide explanation for future problems and failures and help make the administrator more sympathetic.

Care must be taken, however, not to become a habitual complainer. Such behavior will only alienate you with the administrator. Continually blaming classroom difficulties on one aspect of the classroom environment that has been deemed unchangeable may cause you to lose much administrative support. Administrators would rather see teachers trying to positively solve problems rather than always using those problems as an excuse for ineffective teaching. Thus, your willingness to be a team member, while striving to overcome obstacles positively, will enhance your chances for successful teaching experiences and classroom management.

Throughout this chapter we have worked with the physical characteristics of the school setting in trying to show you how to avoid problems and maximize your opportunities for teaching success. The following chapter will be concerned with personal and attitudinal characteristics of your students. We will discuss how your class' group dynamics will also help you achieve your educational goals.

1.   Consider the following situation: You have just been hired for your first teaching position. You are assigned to teach history and English to seventh through ninth grade remedial students. Due to lack of classroom space on the old and overcrowded campus, your classroom, you learn to your chagrin, is actually an unused nurse's office in the "old" wing. Its creaky iron door and darkly painted, chipped interior make it resemble a medieval dungeon. The dimensions of the room are ten by fifteen feet, leaving space for one long library table with chairs around, a teacher's desk, a portable bookcase and portable chalkboard, but no bulletin boards. What would you do to make this room into a classroom that students would enjoy coming to?

The teacher actually confronted with this room did the following.

a. The furniture was arranged in the following way:

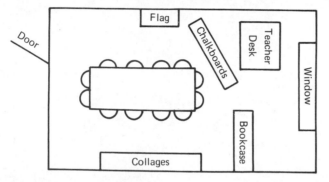

b. Although space was extremely limited, the portable bookcase and chalkboard allowed the room to be separated into two areas—student work space and an office area that could be used for giving individual assistance away from the group. The individual student desk was used for a time–out area. A disruptive student could be removed from the group and the bookcase kept the student from seeing or being seen by others.

c. The work table made the group work as a unit and was good for group discussions and overseeing the students' progress in assignments.

d. Each of the three grade levels made an eleven–foot collage of pictures cut out of magazines and pasted on butcher paper that showed their different interests and brightened up the room considerably.

e. The eighth grade group decided that the room needed an American flag, so they painted a three by five foot flag on butcher paper and taped it to one wall.

2

2. You have been given carte blanche to furnish a classroom in whatever way you feel would best fit your students' needs. List what furnishings you would choose for your ideal classroom and draw the furniture arrangement in the space provided.

Dewey, John, quoted from "Classroom Management," *Professional Growth for Teachers,* 9, No. 2 (1963), p. 1.

Hewett, Frank M., *The Educationally Disturbed Child in the Classroom.* Boston: Allyn and Bacon, Inc., 1974.

Jones, Frederick H., "Teachers and Teaching," *Education Summary,* August 15, 1978, pp. 6-7.

4 Understanding Classroom Dynamics

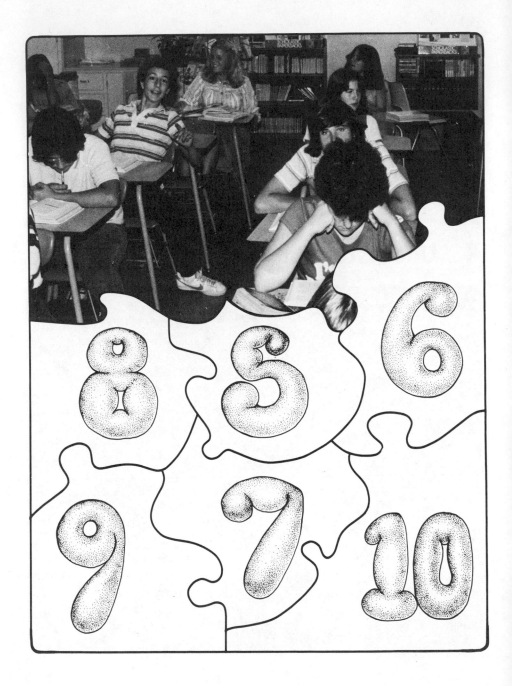

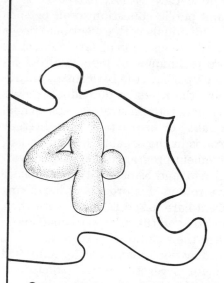

Groups consist of individuals, it is true, but they are more than just so many people. They develop something like a personality, a "spirit" of their own. They develop some power within them, something upon which their functioning will depend a great deal, something that goes beyond the individuals who constitute them. In a group whose spirit or morale is high, many an otherwise weak individual will be spurred on to better and more efficient performance. In a group whose morale breaks down, even individually well-meaning members will eventually become indifferent or ineffectual.

George V. Sheviakov

Interest in the growth and development of the individual has become a major concern of educators today. Public Law 94–142, passed in 1975, calls for extending the right to free and public education to all persons (including all handicapped persons or individuals with exceptional needs as they are presently called). Consequently, teachers in all levels and of all subjects are including more and more techniques of individualized instruction in their teaching programs to help insure the betterment of education for all. As this interest in serving the needs of individuals grows, pressures are being exerted upon teachers, administrators, and school districts in general, to improve the quality of instruction, raise literacy levels, and strengthen discipline programs in the schools. In some areas, as illustrated by the 1978 parent involvement program directed by Reverend Jesse Jackson in Los Angeles, Chicago, and Kansas City, parents are also being asked to take a more active role in this process of improving education. In Jackson's program, parents are asked to make sure their children do two hours of homework nightly and themselves to make more frequent visits to the schools to monitor their children's progress.

Thus, we are hearing two calls in education today—one for improved and extended individualization and one for increased control, structure or conformity. The coexistence of these two conditions is possible, but cannot be accomplished without a great deal of thought and work. The demands of the somewhat paradoxical classroom social structure require you to strive to maximize each individual's education while working within a group structure. Your students are members of a group and as such cannot be viewed as completely separate entities. Thus, while you are interested in the individual, you must also deal with the group, a fact that greatly complicates the process of individualization. You will have goals for the individuals as well as goals for the group as you design activities to help your students learn and even excel.

The achievement of individual and group goals will be determined in great degree by how well you motivate the individuals within the group to participate in learning activities. While some students like school, you, and your class, and will easily accede to your wishes, you cannot hope to have all students be so enthusiastic about being in your class. The individual attitudes, personalities, and abilities of your students will make teaching both interesting and difficult. An added complication is the fact that when individuals form a group, that group will also have a distinct personality. This group personality has attitudes and interests which may in turn affect the behavior of the individuals within the group. Your successful channeling of their individual energies and establishment of constructive student–teacher relationships will be the key element in achieving the goals you have set both for individuals and the group. For this reason, we are devoting this chapter to a study of group dynamics and the effects your knowledge of your class' social climate have upon your preparation of the best possible learning environment for your students. Such knowledge will help you minimize personality clashes while maximizing group cohesiveness and individual growth. This is done by understanding your class' group dynamics and by using this knowledge to serve your students as well as yourself in the classroom.

The Whats and Whys of Group Dynamics. Whenever you teach more than one child at a time, you are dealing with a group. Although groups may vary in goals and individual makeup, they share at least one thing in common—that the situation is influenced to a significant degree by certain members of the group, the group leaders. Whenever individuals join a group, their actions and subsequent duties reflect their role or status within the group's social structure. Groups need leaders who initiate actions, assist in decision making, and through their strengths, hold the group structure together. Groups also need the workers (or followers) who follow instructions, persevere, and work together to achieve the goals of the group. This role assignment of individuals within the group is not static and changes in accordance with the needs of the individual or group. Role assignment then is as much a function of the individual personalities of the group members as it is of the group's need for organization. Groups work the way they do out of necessity. An organized group of individuals is capable of producing much more efficiently than a group of nonrelated persons working separately.

Your students also will function according to the goals, needs, and interests of their group. Their needs for friendship, social conformity, entertainment, and intellectual stimulation and learning will greatly affect their classroom behavior. While you, as a teacher, are the main group leader in the classroom, your leadership will be affected by the amount of cooperation you receive from the student peer group leaders. This will become especially apparent as the students near adolescence and increasingly seek independence from family ties and adult authority figures. This situation is so important that your success in establishing rapport and effective student-teacher relationships may be gauged by your ability to overcome peer group opposition to your goals and methods.

The Importance and Recognition of Group Leaders. Being hired as a teacher does not automatically make you the only director of classroom affairs. A major goal of teaching is to facilitate learning. This is not necessarily accomplished, however, by the teacher leading all activities. Possibly the best form of learning occurs when the students voluntarily take the lead in learning activities that have been properly organized for maximum benefit for them by their teacher. In order to activate and maintain such voluntary student-motivated learning, the teacher has to carefully structure the classroom environment in such a way that both school goals and student desires are integrated and achieved. This can be most successfully accomplished when you enlist the aid of your student peer group leaders. Your ability to instruct your students and maintain discipline will be greatly dependent upon your ability to analyze the class social structure, determine which students lead their peers to action and encourage those leaders to positively participate in class activities.

Recognizing leaders is not always an easy task. The group leader is not always the seemingly best-liked student in class. Although a student is extremely popular among his peers, he or she may not necessarily command their respect or lead them to action. When trying to maintain your leadership and decrease classroom behavioral problems, you must learn which student, if any, is undermining your efforts to the greatest degree. This student's power is not always overtly present in the class. It may grow from student interactions outside of the classroom, when students are not as closely supervised. It often grows from and is manifested by things the teacher does not see. Respect for such a leader grows at recess, between periods, during lunch, and before and after school. A group leader's silence and nonparticipation in classroom activities will be even more powerful than a nonleader's boisterous acceptance or rejection of your plans.

Peer group leaders can be both positive and negative. An example of a positive leader is one who participates in the class lessons and stimulates the participation of the rest of the class members. A negative leader, on the other hand, interferes with learning and the involvement of the rest of the class. Negative leaders are not single-dimensional and do not fit in any single description. They are not always the "class bullies or clowns." They are the ones who continually put a damper on the group's enthusiasm by questioning and criticizing what is going on in the classroom. Some common complaints are:

"We've done this before. Why do we have to do it again?"

"This is boring!"

"This is baby stuff—we did this last year!"

Possibly the hardest one to take is, "Mr. So-and-So's class was more fun than this one!" Too often these criticisms, founded or not, will help to initiate a chorus of "Me-too's" and "Yeah's" from most of the rest of the group. The ensuing discussion of the merits of the activity in question interferes with learning and may lead to teacher insecurity. If the teacher changes or stops the lesson due to this inteference, the negative leader's goal of attaining attention and impeding learning is reinforced and the interference is likely to occur again. Thus, dealing effectively with such a leader is imperative if the teacher's educational program is to flourish. Since any class may have both positive and negative leaders at the same time, the successful teacher must reinforce the positive leaders and lessen the effects of the negative ones. To do this, you must first determine who the leaders are and under what circumstances their leadership occurs. Second, you must interest these leaders in participating fully in your instructional program. Leadership status is determined by teacher observation and careful use of sociometrics. The second strategy is accomplished by applying the knowledge you have gained from your observations of student behavior and sociometrics to help you establish effective and positive student-teacher relationships.

Teacher Observation. We stated in Chapter 2 that the history contained in cumulative records or teacher lounge conversations are poor indicators of what your students will do in your classroom. This is especially true in the area of student interactions. Class membership and personality composition does not remain static year after year. As families move in and out of the area, the addition or loss of persons in your class' social structure will greatly affect how the students relate to each other and to you, the teacher. Even if you teach in a one-room schoolhouse and people rarely move to or from the area, your class will change from year to year. Students mature or have experiences that change their feelings about school, teachers, and learning in general. Thus, records of past student histories will not help you predict how your students will behave in your classroom with a new or changed group of personalities. Since students will not respond to all teachers in the same way, previous teachers' recitations of how particular students behaved in their classes will have limited value for you.

What you *can* count on is your own observations of what actually happens in your classroom. You can see which students other classmates choose to sit with when you have not assigned seats. You can note which students are generally elected to positions of authority *by their peers.* You can spot which students most closely approximate the mode of dressing, hair styling, which is the ultimate in the "in-look" of their particular social group or grade level. Also you can easily tell which student goes out of his or her way to avoid the "in-look." Such overt nonconformity could be the sign of a very powerful student—one not afraid to challenge the existing student social order. When classroom disturbances occur, you can try to notice if one student is always involved in some way. As you watch your students interact in class and out, you can surmise which students are leaders. If the effects of their leadership are positive, you know they are positive leaders and negative effects denote negative leaders. At times, however, the exact source of inappropriate student behaviors is hard to discover, especially when a small *group* of students within the large group seems to be responsible for the behavior. Pinpointing the source of leadership within this small group will help you deal with the inappropriate behavior of the total group. It is much easier to try to change one student's disruptive behavior than it is to change the behavior of a group. A reliable source of information in this matter can be drawn from the students themselves by using sociometric testing.

Sociometrics: A Tool for Analyzing Group Dynamics

Mapping Social Relationships with the Sociogram. If, despite your own close observation of student behaviors, you are still unsure of which student is the strongest positive or negative leader in the class, you may need to turn to sociometrics for additional information. Sociometry, which literally means social or companion measurement,[1] was developed in 1934 by J. L. Moreno in his work, *Who Shall Survive?* Since that time, researchers in group processes have frequently used this tool to determine "the degree to which individuals are accepted in a group, for discovering the relationships which exist among the individuals, and for disclosing the structure of the group itself."[2] The procedure of sociometric testing is quite simple and consists of asking each member of a group to name which of the other group members he or she would prefer to do things with in a variety of situations. Both the mode of questioning as well as the selection of questions must be appropriate to the group under study. For example, students in the primary grades (K-3) should be interviewed informally and individually by the teacher; while students in grades 4–9 can signify their choices by writing their answers on prepared survey sheets.

The type of questions you ask should also be appropriate to the interests, grade level and possibly, sex of the students questioned. Since you want their responses to mirror their actual feelings, you need to ask questions that will as closely as possible mirror their real-life experiences. Basically, you should ask questions that are aimed at discovering who each student would prefer to be with during both fun and work times. From watching and listening to them, you should have a good idea of what your students like to do for fun both in school and out. By carefully choosing from those activities and including important or upcoming classroom activities, you can learn about your students' preferences for companions and from this information infer possible leadership choices. Due to the widely varying interests of individual classrooms of students across the country, we feel that listing samples of questions would not be too valuable for you. However, the basic format of the question is:

Who do you like to sit next to during [reading]?

The choice of the activity in the bracket is up to you and dependent upon what you feel is most appropriate for your class grouping. Another

---

[1] Norman E. Gronlund, *Sociometry in the Classroom* (New York: Harper and Brothers, 1959), p. 1.
[2] Mary L. Northway, *A Primer of Sociometry,* 2nd ed. (Toronto: University of Toronto Press, 1967), p. 3.

type of question is: Which person in our class do you most like to play with at recess (or be with at lunch—for the older students)? In order to keep your motives from being transparent to your students, we feel that including other questions, such as what is your favorite color, food, TV show, subject, book, music style, etc., is a good idea. From such inquiries, you will gain insight into your students' likes and dislikes. Your students will like the fact that you are trying to learn more about them as people, not merely about their friendships.

The students' responses to your questions can be noted or charted in a number of ways, perhaps the most common being the sociogram, which is actually a picture of the group's social choices. A sociogram can be most useful to you when you are unsure which student is the actual leader of a powerful subgroup of students in your class. In the sample sociogram presented in Figure 4.1, each student in such a group is represented by a circled number. Each arrow represents the choice made by the students when asked the following question: "If you had to be transferred to another class, which student would you want to go with you?"

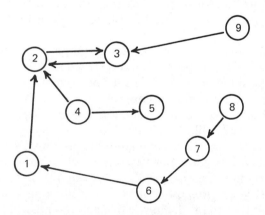

Sample Sociogram   Figure 4.1

From this sociogram of a class subgroup, you can see that Student No. 2 was chosen most often and is the likeliest leader. You can also see that Student No. 2 and Student No. 3 may have the closest relationship (at least under those circumstances and at the time the sociometric test was administered). Naturally more than one question will give you a more valid measure of leadership. Generally three sociometric criteria (situational questions) with three student choices each (three persons that they choose to be with in order of preference) will give a more valid appraisal of who leads under what circumstances.

Thus, the information gained from your sociometric testing can help you to pinpoint the exact source of leadership in your classroom—those students who will motivate the rest of the students through example as much as by command. Now, with the knowledge you have gained from your own observations and/or sociometric testing, you are ready to improve your classroom disciplinary structure by enlisting the cooperation of your student group leaders.

Using Group Dynamics to Establish and Restore Classroom Order

Getting Student Leaders on Your Team. Once you know who the positive and negative leaders are, your real work is still ahead of you. You must coordinate the leadership efforts to help prevent disciplinary disturbances in the classroom. Your gaining the approval of even the most negative leader will be greatly dependent upon your ability to let that student (as well as all others in your class) know that you care for him or her as a person and want each student to benefit to the greatest extent possible from the learning environment in your classroom. How this is to be accomplished will greatly depend upon the level of communication that you have with your students. The better your students understand how much you value them as human beings and the education they will receive in your classroom, the more you will be able to work through difficult times or situations.

The wise teacher will prize the individual personalities of his or her students. When their individual characteristics lead to disruptive group behavior, you should look for any signs of positive involvement that they may show. Encouraging or reinforcing the positive behaviors of your students will eventually lead to diminished or less frequent negative behaviors. Leaders basically like to lead. Thus, if you give students the opportunity to demonstrate their leadership in constructive ways, they will be more likely to become positive leaders. Care must be taken, however, to avoid reinforcing the negative leadership of students. Making your negative leaders more powerful by disproportionate or misplaced encouragement will lead to producing a stronger and possibly more negative influence in the classroom social structure. Equally important to avoid is belittling negative leaders. If you try to control leaders by making them look foolish or less important, you are actually saying to the whole group that their choices are without worth. The best approach is to look for positive qualities and reinforce them whenever they occur.

One example of reinforcing the negative leaders' positive behavior that a junior high school teacher tried grew out of a social studies activity that was outlined in American Education Publications unit book, *Political Parties in the U.S.*[3] The activity, called the Party Game, was aimed at teaching students how political parties are developed. Campaign issues

---

[3] *Political Parties in the U.S.* (Middletown, Conn.: American Education Publications, Xerox Corporation, 1968), pp. 4–5.

arose from such student interests as student participation in curriculum selection. Such issues were analyzed, voted on, students assigned to political parties on the basis of their choices, and party recruitment headquarters set up to try to swing voters over to the various parties' ways of thinking. The group or party with the greatest number of points at the end of timed recruitment rounds was the winner. The teacher in this example, concerned by her class' group dynamics and the behavior of one negative leader in particular, decided to use this interesting game to give her student leader a positive outlet for his leadership tendencies. She modified the exercise in that she chose campaign issues which specifically grew out of her students' classroom concerns. She assigned predominantly positive issues to a particular party's leader (who was also the class negative leader). Then she assigned another well-liked student who was perhaps a little less powerful in terms of group dynamics to head the other group. The resultant planning, poster–making, and debates were great fun for the students and the negative leader became actively involved in the whole process. A taste of constructive leadership was very good for this student. He loved being in charge, and his party won the election. Not only was a step taken toward improving this student's behavior, but also all students benefited from an activity in which they had to coordinate the efforts of the total group to accomplish a group goal. In this instance, the teacher accomplished a multifaceted goal by joining her knowledge of group dynamics with curriculum management.

Using group dynamics carefully can improve the behavior of both the class as well as individual students. However, you must exercise extreme caution when working with the dynamics of the group. A heavy-handed approach could result in the social isolates in the class becoming even more isolated. Also, your students might resent your manipulation of their peer group structure and lower their trust and acceptance of you. Whenever you study the group dynamics of your classroom, you must prize the rights of both the group and the individuals of that group and design strategies that will benefit both the group and the individual. Discretion and caution will help you to improve the social climate of your classroom without adverse effects upon the individual students.

People Management—Its Place in your Classroom

Once you have arrived at the point where you feel you and your students are relating well and, with a few minor exceptions, are contributing to the overall success of your teaching and their learning, you may think that your worries about group dynamics are over. Such is not the case, unfortunately. Each additional adult who may enter your classroom, either on a regular or intermittent basis, will affect the social climate in your class.

The presence of ancillary personnel such as speech therapists, reading or math specialists, and volunteers or paid aides, will affect your behavior and your students' behavior. For this reason, care should be taken from the start of any co-teaching, or co-working relationship to make sure that all personnel are aware of classroom rules and procedures. Ancillary personnel who do not know that you want certain student behavior ignored or who disrupt your class' closely-supervised social structure can lessen the effectiveness of your program and change the social structure negatively.

Any outsider entering the group after it has been formed can become a change agent. Hopefully, these changes are for the better, but many times teachers find themselves struggling with new problems, such as students showing off or acting out for the benefit of the new adult figure. Much of this can be avoided if you understand the dynamics of ancillary personnel in the classroom and prepare carefully (when possible) for their visits. This preparation revolves around your sharing your goals and methods with them and discussing their feelings of their place in your program. From this discussion, you should be able to determine potential troublespots or conflicts in your philosophies and plans and work to eliminate most problems before they appear in your classroom. Such tactics will make all involved—teacher, students, and ancillary personnel—much more successful.

Throughout this chapter we have considered the part that interpersonal dynamics plays within your classroom. Interpretation of such dynamics, such as the physical environment previously considered, gives the teacher a good start in viewing the total process of learning that occurs within the classroom. Once again, the successful teacher is the one who tackles problems in a consistent fashion and tries to anticipate and disarm future problems through a process of continuous assessment and well–thought–out interventions. Now that we have analyzed how the people work together in their setting, we are ready to consider the next very important variable—curriculum and its management. The body of learning to be studied in the classroom is not inert material that is just passed from teacher to student with no effects upon the classroom structure. Preparing a curriculum that will improve discipline and maximize learning will be the theme of the next chapter.

Attempting to improve the behavior of all students on the school campus can also be in part accomplished through such planning and concerted efforts toward maximizing communication. Such a program does not occur haphazardly and is only successful if all staff members are committed to working toward its success. One such program was undertaken at an elementary school with a 650 student population. A letter was sent home to the parents explaining the program that was aimed at fostering "independence and responsibility" within the students while teaching them how to deal positively with conflict. The letter, printed with the permission of the Orange Unified School District, follows:

HANDY ELEMENTARY SCHOOL

April 14, 1978

Dear Parents,

As a part of our on-going planning at Handy School, we have been investigating the dependence and independence of the students and seeking ways and means of fostering independence and responsibility with the students. A crucial part of developing responsible independence in our students is to teach them how to deal with conflict and disagreement.

We are implementing a program at Handy School called "Conflict Management." It is designed to help children use positive ways of dealing with conflict when it arises. It works with the other values we have been emphasizing, this year, in developing responsibility and self-reliance.

Conflict is a normal and inevitable part of life. We can expect children to encounter it frequently, but we need to show them positive ways to cope with it. Children need models that demonstrate various positive ways of managing conflict. Unfortunately, there are few models children will pay attention to, which illustrate positive, constructive ways of resolving differences of opinion and conflict. In television drama, a great percentage of the stories show violence as a workable, acceptable method of resolving conflict. How do the heroes resolve the conflicts with the "bad guys?" "Pow! Bash! Bang!" of the Batman show is typical. Even in the news--radio, television, newspapers--physical and verbal violence are the most used means of handling conflict. When children are shown and realize there are many responsible, constructive alternatives available to them, they almost invariably become enthusiastic about using them.

At Handy School we are implementing Conflict Management in the following way: In each classroom at Handy School, the alternatives are discussed and then listed on a chart for the children to refer to. We are also having them painted on a building wall facing the playground so the children can use these alternatives at recesses.

CONFLICT MANAGEMENT [*]

1. Talk it over--Listen.

2. Say, "I'm sorry."

3. Do something else.

4. Take turns.

5. Share

6. Ignore it.

7. Walk away.

8. Ask for help.

---

[*] *A Curriculum on Conflict Management* by Uvaldo Palomares.

The child must try two alternatives from the chart before he asks for help and he must state the two alternatives when asking for help. Example: "Mrs. H., Joey is teasing me. I've tried ignoring him, and talking it over, and he is still doing it." (Obviously, we are not using this if the children are in actual physical danger.)

We hope that you will use these techniques at home. They will help you and be useful to your child his entire life. Your child needs on-going training and practice if he is to internalize these techniques--so that he will automatically seek positive ways of dealing with conflict situations.

Conflict management must become a deliberate and intentional process, a well-developed skill rather than a behavioral area left always to the random emotional decisions of the moment.

We grow by discovering, practicing and doing. The tools are here to help that happen for your child.

Sincerely,

THE HANDY ELEMENTARY SCHOOL STAFF

Conflict Management Reminders in Classroom and Play Areas

Figure 4.2

The entire school was involved in this program. Everyone from noontime supervisors to the principal learned the alternatives of Palomares' "Conflict Management" (see Figure 4.2). Such a program demonstrates how a very large group of teachers, students, assorted staff members, and parents can be coordinated in an effort to try to improve the social/behavioral climate of an entire school campus.

1

1. Consider the following two classroom situations. Decide what techniques included in the two previous chapters should be used to try to solve these problems.

- *Situation No. 1:* You are a beginning junior high school English teacher. Your afternoon class of eighth grade students seems particularly difficult. One of the biggest troublespots seems to be in the person of one really popular student who appears to have a natural aversion to English teachers and English classes. He sits in the back row within four feet of open windows. Whenever you work at the blackboard or become involved in giving individual help, be busies himself by making paper airplane gliders and launching them out the open windows to the grass one story below. If you have a particularly busy period, the grass is sometimes covered with paper airplanes. The custodians bring this situation to the attention of the principal and also mention that the desks in your class are covered with graffiti. The principal speaks to you about these problems and you fear you will receive a poor evaluation if you cannot stop these problems. What do you do?

- *Situation No. 2:* Each morning Andy arrives at his fourth-grade classroom 10 to 15 minutes late. This pattern of behavior is due in part to the intentional detours that he makes during his walk from home to school, and to his dawdling once he gets to school. Your problem is not so much *when* he enters class as *how* he enters the room. Each day he walks into the room, closes the door carefully, stands solemnly and then proceeds to trumpet a fanfare (for himself) of dat-da-da-daaah! On some days he even adds a few flourishes and bows. The students look forward to his daily entrance with great joy. You, however, grow to dread his appearance because it means that each day whatever is happening in the class is going to be interrupted. No matter what you do prior to Andy's arrival, the students are preoccupied awaiting his appearance. On days Andy is absent, the situation is even worse because they sit with one eye on the door until the first recess when they are sure he is not going to show up. Your ignoring this behavior does not work. Neither does suggesting to Andy that he enter class quietly without interrupting the proceedings. You are faced with the prospect of arguing with or punishing this student each day upon his arrival. What should you do?

2

2. A specialist (in reading for elementary and in curriculum for junior high) will be working with less able students in your class while you work with the remainder of the class. What will you need to know about this

person's program before he or she begins? What elements of your class' interpersonal dynamics should the specialist know about before beginning work with your class?

Gronlund, Norman E., *Sociometry in the Classroom.* New York: Harper and Brothers, 1959.

Moreno, Jacob L., *Who Shall Survive?* Washington, D.C.: Nervous and Mental Disease Publishing Company, 1934.

Moreno, Jacob L., *Who Shall Survive?* New York: Beacon House, 1953.

Northway, Mary L., *A Primer of Sociometry* (2nd ed.). Toronto: University of Toronto Press, 1967.

"The Party Game," *Political Parties in the U.S.* Middletown, Conn.: American Education Publications, Xerox Corporation, 1968.

Sheviakov, George V., "The Management of Classroom Groups," *Professional Growth for Teachers,* 9, No. 2, 1963, p. 2.

5   Curriculum Management

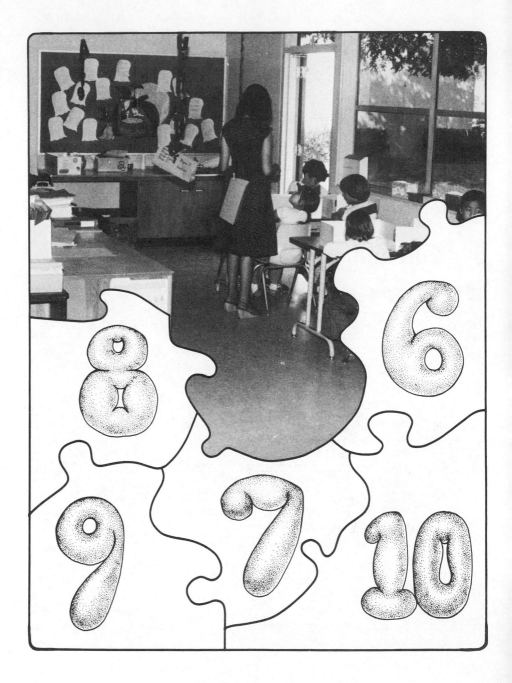

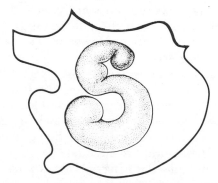

This child is a precious thing. Try to know him [her] well. Bring him [her] into your classroom as a loved and esteemed member of the group. Respect him [her] for what [s]he is and guide him [her] to discover what [s]he can do best. Help him [her] to grow in wisdom and skill. Show him [her] that [s]he has within him [her] a capacity for greatness. Give him [her] the will to touch the stars. Protect him [her], and cherish him [her], and help him [her] to become his [her] finest self.

Duane Manning
A Humanistic Curriculum

The sentiment contained in Duane Manning's quotation at the beginning of this chapter states the concern that all teachers should feel for their students' individuality and welfare. Such concerns and the teaching strategies and student learning that evolve from them are the crux of the teaching/learning process. Although school districts hire specialists to determine what *should* be taught in the schools, it is the teacher who determines what *is* taught in the classroom. The individual teacher has immediate contact with each and every student and is in the best position to determine what each student needs to learn to achieve that "capacity for greatness," or maximum potential. Your decisions of how they will best learn will be influenced greatly by your own philosophy of curriculum planning and will in some way be aligned with one of the two dominant psychological theories of contemporary education: behaviorism or humanism.[1] Despite reams of material printed on how behaviorism and humanism differ and careful lists of the merits and/or disadvantages of each, we do not feel that teachers should cling to either extreme, overlooking the possible value that the opposing view has to offer for the individual teacher and student.

For years, the authors of this text have been referring to themselves as humanistic behaviorists (and we hardly feel schizophrenic at all). We are very much concerned with the individual growth, perceptions, and personal reality of each student. However, we are also concerned with how individual actions and attitudes may interfere with learning growth of the individual and other members of the group. When such interference occurs, we feel the teacher must manage the total learning situation in order to improve the chances for growth and learning for all.

Although the distinction between behaviorism as training and humanism as education has been made,[2] we do not feel that they are mutually exclusive. Behavioral techniques can possibly improve the humanistic program; and the behavioristic teacher cannot be truly successful if unresponsive or insensitive to the needs of students. Our program of anticipative action is built upon the merging of these two philosophies. Humanism helps you to learn about your students and to reach out to them and communicate. Behaviorism supplies the means for improving the quality of their education, providing a structure that can help you to deal with disciplinary problems that may be interfering with individual growth. Whether you want your students to be "intrinsically motivated" (humanistic model) or "to establish voluntary control over their own behavior" (behavioristic model), you are talking about the same thing, your students participating voluntarily in the learning process and following the rules of appropriate conduct that have been established by

---

[1] Walter B. Kolesnik, *Humanism and/or Behaviorism in Education* (Boston: Allyn and Bacon, Inc., 1975), p. v.
[2] Robert S. Zais, *Curriculum: Principles and Foundations* (New York: Thomas Y. Crowell Company, Inc., 1976), pp. 316–319.

you or the school community at large. Simply stated, we feel that behavioral techniques can be employed successfully to achieve humanistic goals within a program of curriculum management. Such a program is the subject of the remainder of this chapter.

The Teacher—A Manager of Curriculum

We stated in the introduction of this text that student behavior or misbehavior does not occur in a vacuum, isolated from all that happens around it. Learning in the classroom is the result of many complicated and interrelated factors. Student interest, abilities, knowledge, and motivation combine with teacher knowledge of subject matter, students, and methodology to contribute to the success or failure of the total learning program. Once again, the teacher is a manager. You are the one who implements state, school district, and school guidelines by managing these diverse elements to maximize your students' learning. This total process, curriculum management, is the heart of the operation of teaching. The degree to which student misbehavior impedes this process is a measure of teaching ineffectiveness. Interestingly, the complete reverse of this statement is also true. Your successful management of curriculum will decrease student disciplinary problems and thus increase your total teaching effectiveness.

At the end of Chapter 4, we showed how a teacher combined knowledge of group dynamics and the selection of subject matter to try to improve student behavior and discipline. In this chapter, we will carefully examine the components of this vital process of curriculum management. Going beyond lesson planning, we will consider the importance of student behavior, as well as teacher behavior, in the instructional/disciplinary structure of curriculum management.

Common Discipline Problems Which Interfere With Learning

Disruptive individuals (particularly if they are student peer group leaders) can seriously affect the functioning of the classroom instructional program in a number of ways. Such disruptive students can interrupt individual lessons and whole units of study by criticizing content, the mode of presentation, and its relevance to the students' lives. If their peers accept these criticisms as valid, such students can stop learning in the class while the teacher struggles through long discussions of why education has to be this way, or why this or that subject is important to learn.

Teachers who too often find themselves dealing with such disruptions will often choose to stay with one mode of study, such as having the students read a chapter independently, answer study questions, and take quizzes and tests to demonstrate their acquired learning. For them, more dynamic methods of study are to be avoided for a variety of reasons. Discussions, debates, and oral reports are impossible if students interrupt, change the subject repeatedly or talk among themselves. Small study groups are impossible if students are so busy talking among themselves that the assignments are not heard, understood, or completed. Independent study, utilizing high-interest media (such as film strips, tapes, computers, self-correcting or individually-monitored machines), is not possible if students are destructive or misuse equipment. In such situations, curriculum is in danger of becoming static and uninteresting, and thus learning can be severely limited. Since an unfortunate accompaniment to uninteresting learning situations is increased disruption among bored students, you must deal effectively with this problem to avoid an escalation of disciplinary problems.

Two-Phase Curriculum Plan for Avoiding Instructional Disruptions

Avoiding such an escalation can be accomplished best by structuring the learning environment, and more specifically, by structuring curriculum, either to make such disruptions impossible or take steps to reduce the likelihood that they will recur. Both avoiding and attacking the problem provide the impetus for anticipative action in teaching. This entire process is marked by organization and assessment and will be outlined in the following discussion of a two-phase plan for curriculum management.

Phase One: Anticipating the Problem

Avoiding instructional disruptions is best accomplished through careful preparation based upon assessment of student needs and interests. Thought should be given to both what they have learned in the past and what they will need to learn in the future. All student disruptions are not due to student "orneryness" or the "desire to drive the teacher crazy." Actually, very few stem from such motivation. More often, student disruptions may be covering up the fact that they do not have the necessary information, abilities, or background to take part in class discussions or to complete assignments. Your students' lack of interest in the subject matter being presented will also generate more disruptions. Student boredom is a natural outgrowth of studying the same subject matter in the same way year after year or week after week. Your decision to review previously studied materials and concepts should be based either on the need for overlearning (e.g., in situations in which the teacher wants to improve their retention of habits, or in which the learning of two similar tasks can be facilitated)[3] or else for providing additional information to clarify mis-

---

[3] Wendell I. Smith and J. William Moore, *Conditioning and Instrumental Learning: A Program for Self-Instruction* (New York: McGraw-Hill, 1966), p. 134.

conceptions or important forgotten details. Such a decision cannot be made justifiably if the teacher does not take the time to evaluate both student knowledge and interests prior to setting up units of study.

Evaluations of this nature will help you to construct a more successful instructional program in which instructionally-based disruptions are minimized if you are flexible in your treatment of students. If, after assessment, you find that some individuals do not need any further review, you may be able to anticipate and avoid future problems with these students by engaging them in activities that will keep them interested, occupied and non-disruptive while the rest of the class is reviewing. Such individualization is not effortless or problem-free. Care must be taken that the activities of either group do not interfere with those of the other. A change from the usual in furniture arrangement, such as was discussed in Chapter 3, may help lower the level of distraction for the whole class. Also, the students who do need review should not be placed in a position wherein they feel they are being punished for their lack of learning or ability. To keep these remaining troops from rebelling while their peers are having fun with supplementary activities, you should provide interesting review activities. Although such preparation may mean additional work for you, we feel that you will be better off devoting this extra time and effort to improving learning activities than you would be using the same amount of time and effort arguing with students or trying to salvage semi-doomed learning lessons. When you do the former, you are using your energies constructively and greatly reducing the potential for development of teaching anxiety states.

If you follow the model just outlined and have discovered what your students need to know—your next concern is to discover under what circumstances they learn the best. Once again, individual differences among students will add a dimension of confusion to your curriculum planning. All persons do not learn the same way. In fact, each person will learn best by one, or a combination of any, of the modes of learning presented in Figure 5.1. Since time and resources do not permit, you cannot possibly present your subject matter in 36 different ways for your 36 different pupils. You can do the next best thing, however; that is, try to use materials that will benefit both your visual and aural learners.

Since using one mode of presentation exclusively will limit your ability to meet your students' needs, you should not design a curriculum that is predominantly one way or another. When preparing supplementary materials, consider which of the modes of learning could most effectively help reinforce vital concepts for your students. This is when bulletin boards become more valuable as educational devices than as decorations. You may be able to prevent many valid, but interrupting, questions if procedures or directions are presented pictorially through previously made charts or examples. This is especially helpful if your assessment of your students or past records indicates that a group or even one student does not respond well to verbal instructions or forgets proce-

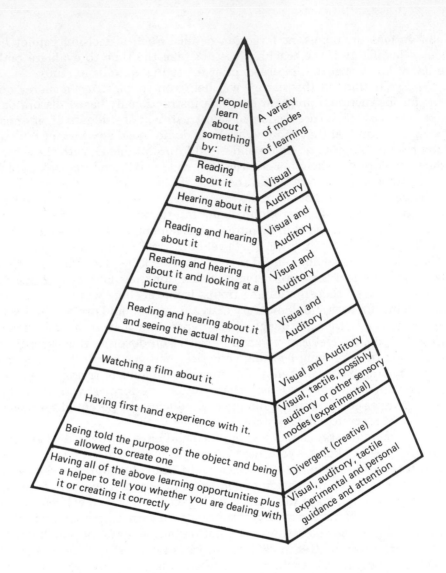

People learn about something by:

A variety of modes of learning

Reading about it	Visual
Hearing about it	Auditory
Reading and hearing about it	Visual and Auditory
Reading and hearing about it and looking at a picture	Visual and Auditory
Reading and hearing about it and seeing the actual thing	Visual and Auditory
Watching a film about it	Visual and Auditory
Having first hand experience with it.	Visual, tactile, possibly auditory or other sensory modes (experimental)
Being told the purpose of the object and being allowed to create one	Divergent (creative)
Having all of the above learning opportunities plus a helper to tell you whether you are dealing with it or creating it correctly	Visual, auditory, tactile experimental and personal guidance and attention

Figure 5.1   Nine Levels of the Modes of Learning

dures. Not having to stop mid-instruction to answer questions that could be answered by referring the student to a chart, overhead transparency, or supplementary ditto will free your time greatly for instructing the group as a whole.

Such time-saving preparations will help you by cutting down on disruptions, but more important, they will help a student who is struggling to keep up to be more successful and to continue to learn within the mainstream of the group. One example of preventing such disruptions is shown in Figure 5.2. It was originally printed in the September, 1977, *Learning*

The drawing on each card depicts an activity scheduled for that day. The cards have a hole punched in the upper left-hand corner in the appropriate order for a given day. They could be rearranged or additional cards added as scheduling was changed.

Memory Jogging Task Cards*   Figure 5.2

Disabilities Guide.[4] The first grade teacher in this illustration had one student who could not remember the sequence of daily activities and his subsequent questions greatly interfered with the smooth running of the class. Her preparing a packet of activity cards to remind him of the daily schedule resulted not only in improving his behavior and chances for success, but also in improving the general functioning of the class.

[4] Cathy Golden, "The First Grader's Memory Jogger," *Learning Disabilities Guide,* Elementary, September, 1977, p. 5.
 * Reprinted with permission of the publisher, Croft-NEI Publications, *Learning Disabilities Guide,* September, 1977, copyright Bureau of Business Practice, Inc.

Phase Two: Organizing the Curriculum

The best intentions in curriculum planning mean little if they are not followed up by well-organized and consistent efforts. If a teacher wants to manage classroom activities rather than be carried along by the flow of student behavior or misbehavior, he or she must try to be as effective as possible. For our definition of effectiveness, we draw from the work of renowned time-management consultant, Alan Lakein, who defined effectiveness as "selecting the best task to do from all the possibilities available and then doing it the best way."[5] This statement, which is easier said than done, defines a very difficult and complex decision-making process that all teachers are involved in as they strive to educate their students. The key element of this process is setting priorities in goal making. Lakein suggests that the ABC Priority System should be used during this decision-making process. In such a system, lists are made stating what things need to be done. Then the listed items are evaluated for their importance. A's are assigned to those items that are most important and must be accomplished first; B's to those of lesser importance and need to be done second; and C's to the least important that are done last. This system can be refined by further evaluating your A's and deciding in order of importance which should be done first and assigning numbers to the A's (A1, A2, A3, etc.).

Such a system helps to keep you from being overwhelmed by the magnitude of tasks which may confront you. You know you cannot teach everything to everyone at once. A priority system will help you to accomplish your educational goals with less worry and wasted effort. You may want to make daily or weekly lists, or you may want to evaluate your priorities in just one area of classroom activity, such as improving classroom communication. Such lists should be collected in one place for easy reference. One time saver would be to mimeograph a *Things To Do* list such as that shown in Figure 5.3 so that you can rapidly set priorities when the need arises. Such lists should then be kept in a file that is easily accessible.

Time Management and Flexibility in Avoiding Instructionally-Based Disciplinary Problems

Priority lists and well–thought–out lesson plans developed from them are the first steps in organizing your educational program. Evaluation of your activities, as well as those of your students, in terms of their importance to educational goals, will help you to manage your total classroom program more effectively. However, as important as lists, plans, and evaluations

---

[5] Alan Lakein, *How to Get Control of Your Time and Your Life* (New York: The New American Library, Inc., 1974), p. 11.

Things To Do

Area of primary concern:_____

Check When
Accomplished

A's:

A1:_____

A2:_____

A3:_____

A4:_____

B's:

B1:_____

B2:_____

B3:_____

B4:_____

C's:

C1:_____

C2:_____

C3:_____

C4:_____

Date:_____

Sample Priority List   Figure 5.3

are, your ability to be flexible in both organization and actions within the classroom may be the true measure of success in teaching. As circumstances change in your class, the values of your ABC priorities may change as one of the B's or C's gains in importance. To be successful you must be adaptable to new circumstances, able and willing to make changes in your plans and activities when necessary, either to accomplish your major goals or to facilitate learning in a particular activity. This is especially true when you are trying to deal with student behavior which is disrupting your instructional activities. While keeping your priorities in mind, you must be prepared to move quickly from one activity to another when an activity is seriously foundering. The value of staying with a troublesome activity (e.g., one in which disruptive student behavior has shaken your confidence to the point where you are not sure of your facts or where the classroom discussion or activity is going) or leaving it for a while until you can regroup or prepare better, must be determined quickly and appropriately. When you do decide to stop an activity, you must do so without reinforcing interrupters for their disruptive behavior. In other words, if the goal of your students (they may not have written lists and priorities but they do have goals in mind in a given situation) is to disrupt the proceedings and monopolize your time to avoid an upcoming unpleasant activity, you should not stop your activity and then begin something else they love to do. You should either move to an alternate activity of neutral value or, if possible, directly into the unpleasant activity that they tried to avoid. Such changes should be initiated confidently, not defensively, because, after all, you are the classroom manager and in the best position to know when it is time to change plans.

Time management is the outgrowth of how priorities are dealt with in your particular learning structure. You must be flexible in determining how long activities should last and when activities should be scheduled. If your classroom program is completely individualized, you will have the potential for maximum flexibility in time management. Adapting your circumstances to the demands of student needs will help to make your learning environment more successful and academically-based disruptions fewer. If you learn either through assessment and/or experience that not all of your students are able to "get into" math the first thing in the morning, then it would be better to either schedule such an activity at a different time for the whole group or implement variable scheduling for certain activities so that students can work on different activities at differing times throughout the day. The more options for flexibility that you have, the more you can use time to your and your students' advantage. If you find that the half-hour you had scheduled originally to complete an A activity is insufficient, you may justifiably decide to give your students more time to complete their projects. Lines must be drawn, however, at how much the time should be increased. If one-hour projects frequently grow into three-hour projects, preventing the accomplishment of other important A's, then you should determine who is consuming so much time, whether this consumption is justified and whether you can do anything about preventing such a situation in the future.

Anyone who has ever sat in a classroom for any period of time will most likely have seen the situation portrayed in the cartoon in Figure 5.4. This fairly common practice can be referred to as time-snatching. A few seconds stolen here and a few minutes there can add up quickly during a school day. In some classrooms, time-snatching is so prevalent that a significant amount of time and effort is wasted while the teacher tries to answer endless questions.

There are four basic types of time-snatchers:

1. questioners who don't hear or understand directions

2. questioners who don't have sufficient understanding of subject matter

3. questioners who cannot work independently due to lack of skills

4. questioners who change the subject or ask about nonrelated teacher interests in order to avoid work or to gain your attention.

A teacher who wants to minimize such interruptions must decide on how such questions either can be eliminated or answered quickly without interfering with the group's proceedings and learning. This is *not* done by squelching your students, making them afraid to ask questions. It is accomplished by improving your instructional/disciplinary environment, intervening with strategies that will eliminate inappropriate questions and time-snatching and start time-saving.

Improving the Clarity of Your Directions

The first group of time-snatchers, the ones who ask questions because they do not hear or understand directions, can be dealt with by improving the clarity of your directions and the environment in which they are given. Your mode of giving directions should be analyzed if many of your students fall into this category. Do you speak loudly enough? Is there noise or conflicting activities, such as passing out materials while instructions are being given? Should you use supplementary aids, such as charts, dittos or task cards described earlier in the chapter? Will repeating instructions or taking more or less time for introduction help?

Figure 5.4

Example of Time-Snatching

© 1978 United Feature Syndicate, Inc.

Your effectiveness in directing your students' activities will greatly determine whether your students will be able to successfully participate in the activities. Students will not be able to complete assignments correctly unless they understand exactly what you want them to do. For this reason, as much attention should be paid to your manner of giving directions as is paid to your entire instructional program. If you feel you may be deficient in this respect, you should take steps to improve your direction-giving competency. One easy method is to rehearse your directions ahead of time. By recording what you think you will say, and playing it back, you can easily spot whether your directions are intelligible or confusing. Your rehearsal will show you if your directions are carefully sequenced or whether major steps or procedures are omitted or glossed over. Such practice will improve your level of communication and will result in an improved instructional environment as a whole.

Your students' behavior must also be improved if it hampers the quality of communication in your classroom. Student birdwalking (i.e., wandering off the objective during classroom proceedings) should be discouraged as much as possible. This wastes instructional time as the students lose focus on what they are supposed to be doing. To avoid this, decide the proper sequence of actions, for both teacher and students, that is essential to each individual learning activity. If the students will need to sharpen pencils or find materials, have them do these chores at a time that will not interfere with your verbal instructions. Do not entertain questions such as, "Can I sharpen my pencil?" or "Where are the paper clips?" while you are still explaining what is expected of them. To do so will only serve to confuse other students and will lead to even more questions about what they are supposed to do. Setting up a secretarial skills time, possibly at the beginning of the day or period during which needed materials are gathered, will alleviate some problems in this area. As much as possible, keep your students "on task" during activities. Once again, anticipating possible problems and taking steps to avoid them will help you to improve your total learning program.

The Swiss Cheese Method—
Helping Students to Overwhelm Overwhelming Tasks

Once you have lessened interference from this first group of time-snatchers, you are then ready to work on groups two and three, the ones who question due to insufficient understanding of subject matter or skills. We are all faced with overwhelming tasks in both our personal and professional lives. Time-manager Lakein feels that the best way to deal effectively with such tasks is to turn them into "Swiss cheese"[6] by poking some holes in them. He calls such holes "instant tasks"—the ones that can be accomplished in a few minutes that will eventually lead to accomplish-

---

[6]   Ibid, p. 104.

ment of a major goal or activity. Your structuring of learning activities through task analysis (i.e., the sequential order of related learning steps from easy to difficult) is the way you can help your students to make Swiss cheese out of their seemingly insurmountable school tasks, such as trying to learn things that they are not prepared for, due to lack of either necessary skills or knowledge.

Here your classroom assessment is a valuable aid in establishing this individualized program of curriculum management. After discovering your students' strengths and weaknesses, you are ready to begin improving their chances for learning success. Your assessments are the basis for three types of individualization:

- in structuring learning activities

- in teacher expectancies of student performance

- in evaluation and grading

In an individualized curriculum you develop lessons that will allow even the least able of your students to learn and participate productively. To accomplish this, your students do not have to work only on individual assignments all day long. However, your classroom program must be flexible to allow for the diverse abilities and levels of knowledge among your student population. You can avoid many time-snatching questions if you consider students' individual levels of functioning before making assignments that expect more from them than they are capable of producing. Although one teaching goal may be to complete the state adopted textbook or required units of study, a more important goal is for all of your students to *learn* the important skills or knowledge that is contained therein. This is not done by rushing them along, valuing time more than student needs or feelings. It is done by not expecting as much of the least capable as you do the most capable. It is done by making your students feel comfortable in your classroom, secure in the knowledge that you will appreciate their best efforts no matter how small they are. It is done by providing supplementary learning activities and making allowances for those students who are unprepared to do the quality of work that the most capable can do. Without such preparation, these students would likely fall behind and possibly become even more disruptive.

Student learning is not immediately improved by any single activity. Carefully sequencing steps of learning and not expecting too much from students allows learning to grow gradually, with students participating successfully and at their own pace. You will alleviate many time-snatching questions and blank student looks if you can initiate such a program of curriculum management in your classroom.

In such a program, your students can participate in group activities, but your expectations for their behavior and grading policies should be flexible enough to accommodate all of the individual abilities contained within the group. To do this, you may need to define differing objectives for each student's performance. You should also carefully minimize the variables that are involved in the whole group's participation in the activity.

For example, if you are interested in providing your students with practice in expository writing and are mostly concerned with their ability to state their ideas, do not make the process even more complex by expecting them to spell every word correctly. This will greatly suppress their vocabulary usage because they are capable of using many more words than they can spell. To avoid this problem, you can tell your students that you will be glad to spell any words that they want to use (but may not be able to spell) on the chalkboard. In this way your students' abilities in written expression are not handicapped by their spelling deficiencies. You can work on their ability to spell and look up words in the dictionary in other exercises specifically directed at these skills if they are of concern to you. A crucial decision in curriculum management is whether to combine working toward a number of goals in one activity. This can only be viably accomplished when student production is not dependent upon abilities that they have not completely acquired, as in the above case concerning spelling/writing skills.

In a program where students are being encouraged to do their best, you must also be consistent in your grading policies. It is unfair and demoralizing for students who have been encouraged to try to complete all assignments to be graded only according to group norms and not according to their individual efforts and merits. If you have a student in your class who is continually falling far behind the norm despite your efforts to provide extra practice or a remedial or individualized program, then you should decide whether to refer such a student for special education evaluation and possible placement. You may feel it is advisable to meet with the student's parents or the school counselor or psychologist for additional input before making such a decision. Chapter 8 will discuss how you may most effectively seek help and information from others who are directly and indirectly concerned with your student's educational welfare.

Dealing with Attention-Seeking Questioners

We come now to the fourth group of time-snatchers—the ones who interrupt class proceedings either to avoid work or to gain the attention of the teacher and/or peer group. Although these student disrupters are not directly a product of curriculum-based problems, as were the previous three groups discussed, they are included in this discussion of instructionally-based disruptions because their behavior can seriously alter the effectiveness of the curriculum programs in general. In this instance, the students become curriculum managers in that they have an objective in mind—to gain attention from either the group or the teacher—and they will develop strategies for achieving this objective. *Their* effectivenss is also dependent upon assessment. In this case, the assessment is of the instructor's teaching style, personality, abilities, interests, and needs. Behavioral management can definitely be a two-way street, and the more effective the student is at managing your behavior, the less effective your curriculum or instructional program will be. You can regain your managerial position if you can channel your disruptive student's desire for attention in a positive way. A careful look at curriculum may assist you in doing this. If a student works very hard just to get your attention, you can often get him or her to work harder or discontinue interrupting class proceedings by withholding that attention until he or she produces or stops disrupting others. If disrupters seek the attention of their peers, then you must use your knowledge of the class social structure to plan positive class activities which will help them to gain recognition and attention through positive production without disruption.

Throughout our discussion of curriculum management we have tried to show how your students can be moved to improve their behavior and participate more freely and effectively in classroom activities. We have talked about individualization and the need for assessment and making allowances for individual differences within your instructional program. We have talked about a number of things you can do if your students have shown they do not want to work, or are unprepared to work or cooperate. The final topic to be discussed in this regard is how you can use a well-planned curriculum to motivate your students, to get them to voluntarily and happily want to participate in classroom activities. This is done quite simply—by making learning fun, an experience that none of them want to miss.

Many disciplinary problems in the classroom would not have the chance to occur if the students were engrossed in learning activities. Students who are absorbed in learning are not likely to do anything that will jeopardize their participation in a fun activity. You can feel excitement like electricity in the air when students enjoy an assignment so much that they eagerly seek to do more. Sustaining this level of excitement and absorption is a difficult task, however, because even the most creative of teachers have a hard time coming up with fresh and exciting slants on the same old subject matter and presentation week after week and year after year. Fortunately for teachers, there are a number of sources of new ideas to draw from each year. Professional magazines and journals continuously present new treatments of subject matter. Also educational material vendors develop and sell interesting new materials and media each year. The most plentiful and inexpensive resource of ideas open to the classroom teacher is his or her fellow teachers. If each of the teachers and student teachers in this country come up with just one new idea each year, millions of new teaching ideas would be abounding in classrooms across the country. The communication and sharing of these ideas among staff members is an easy way to help make everyone's instructional program more dynamic and in so doing, make both teaching and learning fun. Teaching innovations help prevent both teacher and student boredom. An interesting classroom environment can make your classroom a happy place that you enter each day eager to teach and with your students eager to learn. We have included several interesting teacher-made curriculum units or ideas at the end of this chapter for you to consider. If they serve to either enrich your existing curriculum or stimulate your thinking in new areas of curriculum development, we feel that we have provided a small public service for teachers and students.

Curriculum management is the total process of carefully balancing concern for appropriate student behavior with concern for appropriate student learning. Content and your structuring of content cannot become such a consuming interest for you that you overlook the effects of your students' behavior. On the other hand, you really cannot think only in terms of reinforcing small pieces of behavior without considering how your classroom program and subject matter will help prepare your students to be successful in future educational and life experiences. As a curriculum manager, you need to use an anticipative action barometer which will tell you when disciplinary strategies can be used to strengthen instruction and when instructional strategies can be used to strengthen discipline. The two types of strategies, when intertwined in a well-planned curriculum, will help prevent classroom boredom, disruptions, and confusion. A more specific discussion of the development of such strategies will be presented in the following chapter.

1
1.   Tape record yourself giving instructions for a student activity. Evaluate your clarity. Do you think you would have eliminated questions or caused more to be asked?

2
2.   What would you do to avoid the following situation?

You have started a lesson in your junior high class. You are in the middle of explaining what to do. You have asked your students to turn to page 32 in their textbooks to look at an example of what they are to do. At this point, several students say they have left their books at home, in their locker, in the library, on the bus, and in various other places around the campus.

Could you have prevented subsequent problems by:

a. telling students to bring their books in advance of when they are needed?

b. having the forgetful students complete the classroom assignment for homework and do another assignment during classtime?

c. sharing books?

d. sending them off to get their books and rescheduling the activity for later in the period?

What advantages and disadvantages will these solutions have for your class?

3
3.   It is the beginning of the school year. You are new to your school, with 34 students (or 160 spread over five periods if you are a junior high teacher). You need to develop a curriculum for them which takes into consideration group dynamics, time management, objectives and goal–making, lesson–planning and school environment factors. How do you make "Swiss cheese" out of this overwhelming task? What are your priorities? What instant tasks will help you accomplish your goals?

Golden, Cathy, "The First Grader's Memory Jogger," *Learning Disabilities Guide* (Elementary), September, 1977, pp. 4–5.

Kolesnik, Walter B., *Humanism and/or Behaviorism in Education.* Boston: Allyn and Bacon, Inc., 1975.

Lakein, Alan, *How To Get Control of Your Time and Your Life.* New York: The New American Library, Inc. (Signet), 1973.

Lavatelli, Celia Stendler, Walter J. Moore, and Theodore Kaltsounis, *Elementary School Curriculum.* New York: Holt, Rinehart and Winston, Inc., 1972.

Manning, Duane, *A Humanistic Curriculum.* New York: Harper & Row, 1971.

Michaelis, John U., Ruth H. Grossman, and Lloyd F. Scott, *New Designs for Elementary Curriculum and Instruction,* 2nd ed. New York: McGraw-Hill, 1975.

Petty, Walter T., Ed., *Curriculum for the Modern Elementary School.* Chicago: Rand McNally College Publishing Company, 1976.

Ragan, William B. and Gene D. Shepherd, *Modern Elementary Curriculum,* 5th ed. New York: Holt, Rinehart and Winston, 1977.

Smith, Wendell I. and J. William Moore, *Conditioning and Instrumental Learning: a program for self-instruction.* New York: McGraw-Hill, 1966.

Zais, Robert S., *Curriculum: Principles and Foundations.* New York: Thomas Y. Crowell Company, 1976.

AN IMAGINATIVE APPROACH TO LEARNING CENTERS

The Monster Day Unit
By Linda Lavine

The following activity sheet was given to students, grade three, as their map for the monster day unit. They were directed to move to any of the ten monster centers to perform various activities which, when done correctly, allowed them to answer the riddle of each center. Along the way, they did fun things like taking the monster to get a drink of water and eating a monster cookie. Thus, while they were busy reading, answering questions, and following directions, they were having great fun, making this pre-Halloween activity a total success for the teacher and students. The monster that the students colored was a dot-to-dot picture on the back of the monster map.

Any activity tied into a scary monster picture would be appropriate for the centers. Some examples are:

1. Using monster words such as scream, skeleton, skull, blood, ghost, cobwebs, etc.

2. Writing all of the words that can be formed from the name Frankenstein.

3. Having a group of monsters numbered on a sheet and asking the students to add all of the numbers together to find out how many tons they weigh.

Monster Day Worksheet

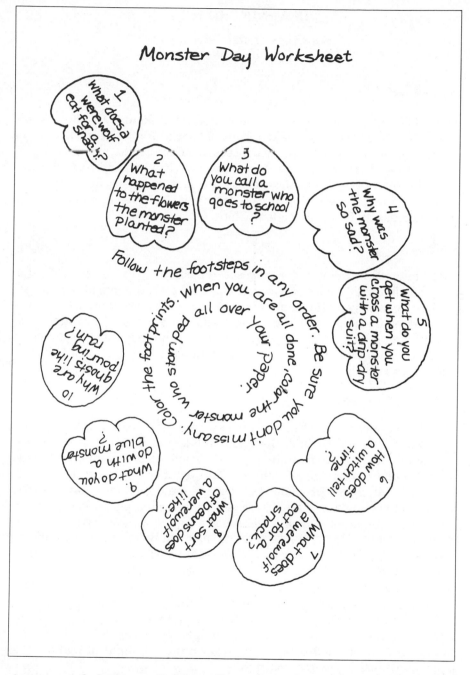

1. What does a werewolf eat for a snack?

2. What happened to the flowers the monster planted?

3. What do you call a monster who goes to school?

4. Why was the monster so sad?

5. What do you get when you cross a monster with a drip-dry suit?

6. How does a witch tell time?

7. What does a werewolf eat for a snack?

8. What sort of beans does a werewolf like?

9. What do you do with a blue monster?

10. Why are ghosts like the pouring rain?

Follow the footsteps in any order. Be sure you don't miss any. Color the monster who stomped all over your paper.

Answers: 1. lady fingers/2. They all gruesome/3. A student/4. Because he tried to kiss his ghoul-friend in the fog and mist/5. A wash and wear wolf/6. With her witch watch/7. Lady fingers/8. Human beans/9. Cheer it up/10. Because they are always in sheets.

LEARNING GAMES

An Open-Ended Gameboard
By Donna Wallis

Objectives

Typical periodic objective for this activity: By excellent 2000, the student will read a list of 250 words taken from Spache's Graded Word List, level 5, with 85% accuracy after three consecutive daily trials.

Typical short–term objective for this activity: By good 2000, the student will read orally from flash cards the first 25 words from Spache's Graded Word List, Level 5, with 85% accuracy after five consecutive daily trials as measured on the Student Chart.

Method

Each student brings his or her own set of flash cards to the game. In this way, individual differences are accommodated and students of wide levels of ability can play in the same game because they use words that have been chosen from their individualized reading programs. They roll one die to move around the board and whenever they land they must read a word correctly. If they miss, they must return to their previous position. The student who finishes first is the winner.

Materials Needed

The Gameboard. After teaching students the sight words with the kinesthetic Fernald method, the open-ended gameboard is used to provide additional practice in a fun way. The teacher has a number of boards so that no more than three children play together at a time (this eliminates many discipline problems because the children do not have to wait so long between turns). The boards can be drawn on poster board, as on page 103, using a popular and well-known figure such as Pete's Dragon or the Incredible Hulk for interest. Or, they can be made out of popular posters (e.g., Star Wars, motorcycle) with paper steps and directions glued on and the entire poster laminated or covered with clear contact paper. They can also be drawn on the outside of file folders for easy storage. Once laminated, they withstand use, abuse, and many moves. The inside of the folder can have a pocket glued on it for holding flash cards or markers. Wrapping papers, cartoons, holiday stickers, Avery dots and pictures from discarded books and magazines are helpful in making the gameboards attractive and colorful.

Boards made for a special story will often spark the interest of a remedial reader. Students can make their own boards by drawing their own routes and deciding their own directions. The teacher can start them out by drawing the control character or illustration and let them go from

Start

Go back to Elliott's finger. Square #2

You're making Elliott's on E ship crash to earth

Elliott is making unhappy sounds and crashes through the schoolhouse wall. Miss 1 turn

The Gogans put in to park

Elliott and Pete are happy because the Gogans fall in tar. Go on to #16

Elliott snorts fire. He saves Pete Skip to #9

Pete is tired Rest here one turn

there. These boards and the word cards can be sent home for play there. Effective practice and drill results from this "fun homework." If there are other children of school age in the home, you can check with their teacher to see if you can make some appropriate word cards so they can play along too. If there are no children, the parents can be called upon to help. They could make up some difficult words for themselves when playing with the child.

Flash Cards. Flash cards could be color coded for groupings or individuals. A handy storage place for sight word cards is the small metal tool chest that has rows of small plastic drawers and is available in most hardware stores. Label each drawer with the child's name on a piece of construction paper using his or her own special color.

The board's usage has no limit because the cards can be made to reinforce knowledge acquired in any classroom activity. For example, flash cards can be made for consonant sounds, blends, vowels, spelling words (by having students skip a space when they are writing their words three times and cutting them apart, they can make their own flash cards), math facts, science questions, geography terms or places. For any activity, make an extra ditto of the facts the class has to learn and cut them apart. Later in the period they can then be used as part of the game. Such games are perfect for use as high–probability activities to be discussed in the next chapter.

Dice. You can make quiet rolling dice out of light weight poster board. They are drawn in the shape below, cut along the dark lines and folded on the broken lines. You can slow the speed of the game by using only numbers one, two, and three on each die.

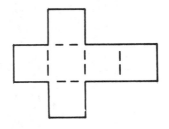

USING CENTERS TO ACCOMPLISH A VARIETY OF OBJECTIVES WITH ONE ACTIVITY

Puppet Making
By Donna Wallis

Goals

To improve psychomotor skills/fine motor, academic achievement: reading skills/oral reading, and self concept/willingness to read aloud to peers or to a younger group of students in a performance.

Methods

After the students have had practice with a variety of cutting experiences with different paper sizes and shapes, the student cuts out a puppet which is to be pasted on a paper sack in the Language Experience center. The student will have a number of puppet forms to choose from. The student then chooses a selection from a basal reader or favorite story and dictates this story to an aide who will type it on a sheet of paper and paste it on the back of the puppet. The student may do this with a friend and/or make two puppets. If there is no aide in your class, the student could print his or her own story on the puppet. More materials can be provided for older students to decorate or dress their puppets more elaborately.

The students can also build their own puppet stage that can serve as a puppet center for the remainder of the year. Have the materials ready so that students who finish an assignment early can productively fill their extra time. A special puppet period at the end of the day or week can be used to display the student handiwork.

Radio Playwriting
By Patricia Howell

This can be used as a substitute for puppet making for junior high students.

Goals

To improve academic achievement: reading (oral), written expression and creative writing, handwriting or printing, and self concept (willingness to perform or read in front of peers), problem solving.

Methods

After students have read, heard recorded radio plays or had several plays read to them, small groups are given a problem to role play. Instead of acting their problems out, however, they first write down (or print) the dialogues and actions they devise on dittos as closely simulating the play format as they can. After the scripts have been mimeographed, they can read them to the rest of the class or into a tape recorder (complete with sound effects). Put into a radio station unit, you can also work in scripts for disc jockeys, records, sports announcers, weather and news bulletins, advertisements, and cooking segments which can all be taped and played back later to approximate radio programming.

Masking Tape Maze
By Robert Howell

Goals

To improve psychomotor skills: either gross or fine motor, and direction following.

Materials

Rolls of masking tape, construction paper.

Method

A maze, similar to the example below (but any shape will do), is taped on the floor using masking tape. This can be done indoors or out, but care should be taken that the floor surface will not be permanently marred by the tape. The students are supposed to complete this obstacle course as quickly as possible. The racers can be started by students waving flags or holding up GO signs. At each square, triangle, or rectangle, new directions are given for the students to follow. Depending upon the abilities or age of your students, these directions can be simple (even pictures if they cannot read) or quite complex. The directions are written on folded pieces of construction paper which the students open as they arrive at each station. The maze in the example is working with gross motor skills. However, fine motor skills can be done at each station such as scissoring or drawing specific shapes. Also, academic skills such as reading sight words or answering math facts can be substituted. The activity can be modified to include any behavior you choose.

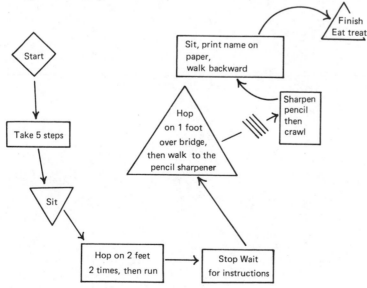

Creative Writing in a Letter-Writing Center
By Donna Wallis

Goal

To improve academic achievement: language/written expression.

Methods

1. Each child designs his own stationery on a ditto. Ten copies are run off for each child to keep. The child can then send home his own notes to parents or brothers and sisters.

2. Since children really enjoy receiving mail, they will eagerly join in activities aimed at this purpose. Using a book such as *The Rainbow Book* by Barbara Haislet, Pat Blakely, ed. (Minneapolis: Parkway Press, Inc., 1976), includes directions on how to send for items as well as lists free items and educational information that they can receive through the mail.

Advertising Unit
By Cathy Thrasher

Goals

To improve academic achievement: writing skills/creative expression both in words and pictures, reading skills, reference skills. To broaden understanding of advertising and consumer practices.

Methods

The following unit was designed to be used by junior high students, but could also be used in the upper elementary grades. We have included the mimeographed pages that made up each step of the total project. Discussions about advertising and acquainting the students with the vocabulary terms listed under the heading of Advertising Vocabulary are necessary before the project can be begun. The box, can, and billboard dittos are used by the students to present their product and advertisement that they created.

Advertising Project

Name_____

This project has many small jobs to do. Each one is very important! Go in the order these jobs are listed. ☑ Check each one when you finish it. Use the vocabulary list, class discussion and any advertisements you've seen to help you to do your jobs!!! Use your imagination.

I. Manufacturer

☐ Select your product from one of these six:
   box   can
   1. cereal   4. soup
   2. cookies   5. soft drink
   3. soap   6. cleanser

Write your product here_____

☐ Brand name--catchy name that people will remember:

Write your brand name here_____

☐ Slogan--catchy words that will help people remember it:
   Write your slogan here_____

☐ Container size--be realistic:
   box: Weight_____   can: Weight_____

         Height & Width_____   Height_____

☐ Cost of one box _____   one can_____

☐ Describe your product--include some of these suggestions:

*Nutritional value?_____

*Good taste/flavor?_____

*Sugar coating?_____

*Doesn't get soggy?_____

*Convenient?_____

*Low price?_____

*Smells good?_____

*Color?   Prizes to send for?   Shape?

II. Advertising Agency

Check off each job
when you finish.

☐ Research Department--find out what qualities (SELLING POINTS)
people will look for in your product. What should you tell
them about your product that will get them to buy it? List
three (HINT - Use your manufacturers' product description
to help):

1._____

2._____

3._____

☐ Copy writer--writes the ad after he decides:

☐ Audience--this ad is for teenagers, both boys and girls.

☐ Location of advertisement--check one in both column A
and column B.

A.	B.
☐ Newspaper	☐ Radio ad
☐ Magazine (which one_____)	☐ TV (which program)
☐ Highway billboard	
☐ Store display	

Remember to check two--one in Column A and one in Column B.

☐ Selling points of product to be included in both advertisements (Use your research results to decide these). DON'T
FORGET YOUR SLOGAN.

1._____

2._____

3._____

☐ Techniques used to advertise (use terms 7-26 from advertising vocabulary list). List way and how to find it in
your advertisement. DON'T FORGET YOUR SLOGAN.

1._____

2._____

3._____

☐ Artist and Director

☐ Plan ad--where to put letters and pictures to get
attention.

☐ Write script (30 seconds), choose actors and props.
DON'T FORGET SLOGAN.

Advertising Vocabulary

Name_____ _____

Directions: Define each of the following terms in the space provided.

1. Advertise_____

2. Propaganda_____

3. Audience_____

4. Analyze_____

5. Selling points_____

6. Technique_____

7. "Selling Words"_____

8. Glittering generalities_____

9. Name calling_____

10. Transfer_____

11. Testimonial (famous people say)_____

12. Recommended by an expert_____

13. Plain folks_____

14. Bandwagon appeal_____

15. Snob appeal_____

16. Youth appeal_____

17. Happy family appeal_____

18. Straightforward ad_____

19. Special offer_____

20. Eye appeal_____

21. Symbol_____

22. Something new_____

23. Humble approach_____

24. Statistics_____

25. Ecology/public service_____

26. Sex appeal_____

Directions: Think up slogans for the following products

Name_____

Soup

    1. USA American Soup_____

    2. Smart Soup_____

    3. Banana Soup_____

Soft Drink

    1. Slikey_____

    2. Mountain Mix_____

    3. Fuñada_____

    4. Super Jet_____

    5. Zippy Wild Cactus Juice_____

    6. Wizz_____

    7. Mother Fletcher's Super Juice_____

Soap

    1. Drive_____

Cereal

    1. Slim Trim_____

    2. Olympic_____

    3. Whooping_____

Cookies

    1. Smiley_____

    2. Joker_____

    3. Pillsbury_____

    4. Dino_____

    5. Football Cookies_____

Sound Familiar?

Directions: #1-9: Identify the product. #10-13: Write down the
             slogan for the product. #14: Think of an additional
             product and the slogan that goes with it.

Slogan

1. Fly the friendly skies   _____

2. The uncola   _____

3. Let US join you.   _____

4. You deserve a break today.   _____

5. Does she or doesn't she...
    Only her hairdresser knows for
    sure.   _____

6. You've come a long way, baby.   _____

7. M'm! M'm! Good   _____

8. Breakfast of champions   _____

9. You can be sure if it's   _____

10. _____ Coca Cola

11. _____ Sara Lee

12. _____ Alka Seltzer

13. _____ Colgate toothpaste

14. _____ _____

Characters & Symbols   Product

1. Madge the beautician   _____

2. Josephine the plumber   _____

3. Jolly Green Giant   _____

4. Ronald McDonald   _____

5. Tony the Tiger   _____

6. 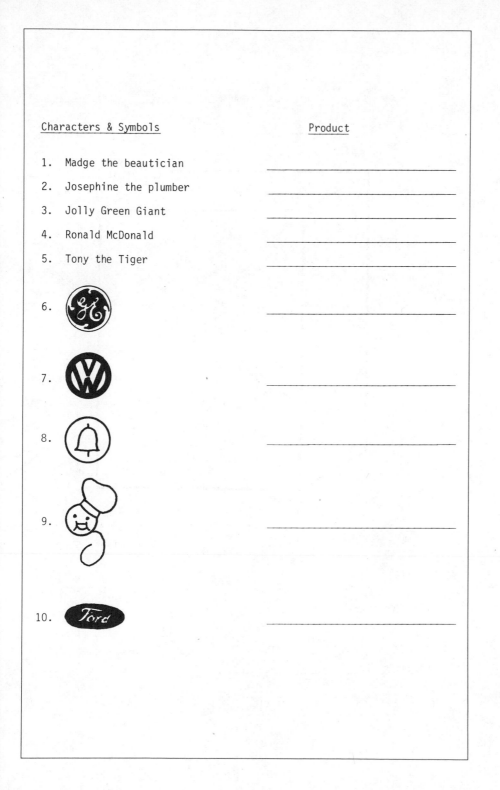   _____

7.   _____

8.   _____

9.   _____

10.   _____

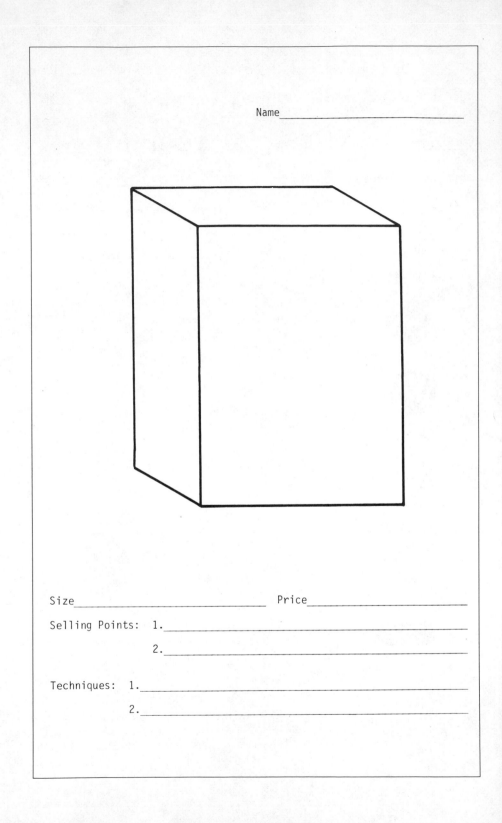

Name_____

Size_____ Price_____

Selling Points: 1._____

                 2._____

Techniques: 1._____

             2._____

Name_____

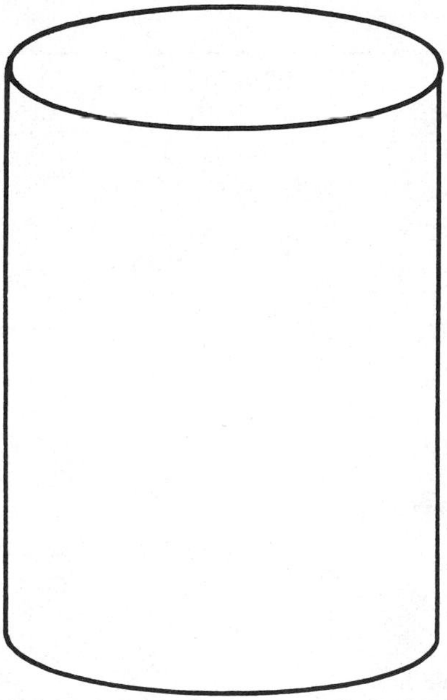

Size_____ Price_____

Selling Points: 1._____

2._____

Techniques: 1._____

2._____

117

Name _____

Billboard   Newspaper   Magazine   Store Design

Selling Points: 1._____

                 2._____

Techniques: 1._____

             2._____

118

6 Constructing a Positive Teacher-Controlled Classroom

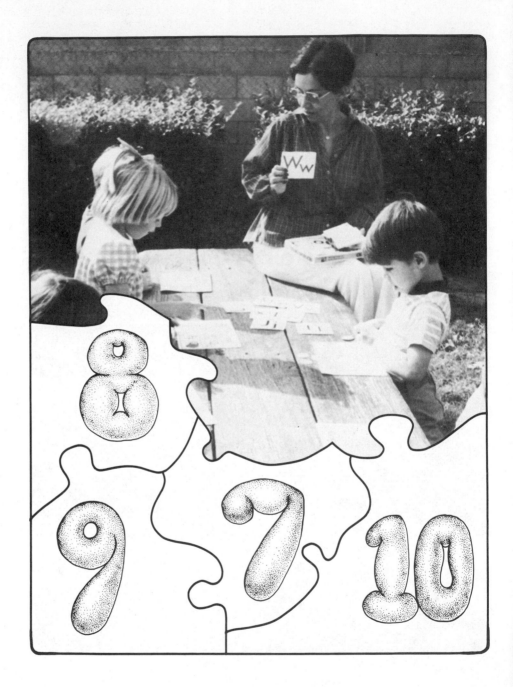

Mr. Flotz was hired to teach school in Virginia City, Nevada, in the 1860's. Hearing that his class would be tough to handle, he arrived on the job well prepared. The first time a student whispered, the teacher whipped out a revolver, trained it on the offender and said quietly: "Don't do that again. I never give a second warning."

The Harry Flotz Method of Dealing with Discipline Problems

Schools, teachers, students and disciplinary methods have certainly changed since the 1860's. Although today's teacher might like to use such an authoritarian and straightforward method as Harry Flotz' when they encounter certain difficult disciplinary situations, such practices are unacceptable (not to mention, unlawful) by today's standards. Since brandishing a six-gun is out, you are faced with the problem of trying to devise strategies for dealing with student misbehavior that are more positive in nature, but equally as effective. Up to this point, we have been primarily discussing how to structure the physical, psychological, and educational or curricular aspects of the environment to avoid behavioral problems. It is, however, impossible to structure a perfect trouble-free classroom. By employing the previously mentioned techniques you merely reduce the potential for misbehavior interfering with learning. You do not prevent all misbehavior from occurring.

We must now consider techniques for dealing with inappropriate behavior as it occurs. Before trying to solve a disciplinary problem, as a teacher your must carefully determine what is at the root of the problem, what is bothering you or interfering with student learning. Procedures for defining student misbehavior will be discussed in the first section of this chapter.

Recognizing Misbehavior When It Occurs

Before you can develop a positive program of classroom discipline, including strategies that adequately deal with student misbehavior, you must first define for yourself what constitutes misbehavior in your classroom. This will be a completely subjective definition based upon what you as an individual feel constitutes inappropriate behavior. Teacher expectancies and definitions will differ from classroom to classroom. The designation of a behavior as appropriate or inappropriate is dependent upon who is observing the behavior. The teacher in Room 6 may feel that a student is behaving appropriately when she answers questions or joins in discussion without raising her hand and being called upon to speak. The teacher's objective in this case is stimulating student interaction, participation and spontaneous discussion. The teacher in Room 7, however, may view such behavior as deplorable. Also the teacher in Room 6 may feel that speaking without permission may be inappropriate in other circumstances.

Thus, the determination of behavioral propriety is as dependent upon the circumstances in which it occurs as the attitudes of the person observing it. Before such a determination can be made, you, the teacher, must sit down and define some ground rules. To do this, you will need to answer several questions. First, what behavior do you feel is appropriate in particular circumstances? Can you enforce your standards consistently? Are they realistic? And, will your ideas of acceptable student behavior clash with surrounding teachers, concerned personnel, or administrative practices? This last question is particularly important. You may enjoy having your students participate in animated discussions and lively, sometimes noisy, activities. However, if the teacher next door complains about the noise or the principal feels you are not controlling your students' behavior sufficiently, you may be forced to alter your program and attitudes. When faced with such situations, you will be more able to defend your program if you are aware of your own objectives and have carefully thought through what constitutes appropriate and inappropriate behavior in your classroom.

Throughout your teacher training, you learn what students need to know and how to teach them the information in the area of your specialization. However, when the first day of school starts, no one can be sure of what will really happen. We have certain expectations, but if you really want to be prepared for the first day and subsequent days, you must try to be prepared for what you do not expect to happen. Last–minute changes, late buses, unexpected influx of students, or sick staff members may lead to classroom chaos which is exciting for the students and anxiety–producing for the teachers. Thus, handling the expected and the unexpected is the first order of business. To do this, try to observe what happens in your classroom immediately. Look for who is saying what. Look at how your students react to each other, you, and your plans for the year, if you share them with them.

At this point, you are starting to set your instructional plan into effect. Hopefully, student behavior will not adversely affect your program. However, if you find yourself drawing time away from your instructional program to deal with disruptive student behavior, you must then initiate a disciplinary program that is specifically aimed at eliminating problem behaviors. Assessment is the first step in this process. Once again, you must carefully define what is occurring through close observation. Inappropriate classroom situations such as students acting out, yelling or not complying with your commands, can be simply defined by assessing who was doing what to whom. It is important that you try to know what happened before the mishap, what happened during the incident, and what happened directly after. Learning to observe events in their totality, not just the results or the instigation, allows you to get to the root of the problem and try to deal with it. Disciplining the wrong person is wasted effort and can lead to future problems. Also viewing the event as a whole helps you to determine what motivates the behavior. Often a behavior will seem to pop up out of nowhere. For seemingly no reason a student refuses to do something you ask. At first you might be at a loss to explain this behavior. However, by looking at your own reaction as well as that of the peer group, you may find that the resulting attention is what stimulated such behavior in the first place. Along these lines, a student's being sent to the office or your reporting misbehavior to parents may have been what the student wanted all along. In such a situation, what you think will extinguish an unwanted behavior will actually reinforce it (or make it more likely to occur). Quickly but carefully, you must review the possibilities before you act. Responding without thinking will only serve to increase your student behavioral problems. You may hit on a lucky solution, that is also correct, a few times; but it is more likely that your immediate, unthinking response will not be your best.

Instead of jumping to conclusions, you should follow a two-step program of Teacher Watch and Consult (TWC). As the classroom teacher (T), you watch (W) what occurs to determine who did what. Next you consult (C) with yourself. During this time you review possibilities, look for behavioral patterns and try to determine what would be the most sensible action to take that is also consistent with your total disciplinary approach. TWC gives you a reasonable approach for attacking the problem. After you decide what to do, you then must watch to see the effect of your actions. Hopefully, you have discouraged the misbehavior from recurring. If this is not the case, you must look more closely at the behavioral dynamics of your classroom. One means of doing this, the recording of student behavior, will be discussed in the following section.

Recording Behavior: How and Why

Recording behavior is a mechanistic and time-consuming procedure. However, it is a procedure that can be used to good advantage if your classroom is in turmoil or if you are bothered by some seemingly undefinable aspect of it. It helps you to be aware of what you are dealing with and, in some instances, shows you how your behavior, as well as that of your students, may need to be changed in order to help maintain a desirable instructional atmosphere. If you want to design a classroom in which your students may be successful and enjoy themselves, then you may feel that the utilization of such a procedure is necessary to combat disruptive elements. Like the sociogram, recording behavior gives you a visual picture of what is occurring in your class.

In recording behavior, you do not try to write down everything that happens. You do try to maintain a record of important behavior, either positive or negative, that may be influencing your classroom structure. The behavior that bothers you most should be your primary target. Children not raising their hands, pushing, not following directions, not respecting the rights of others, or any other acting-out behavior may be chosen as the behavior you most desire to change and thus be the focus of the behavioral record.

Before you are able to start your recording, you must first deal with the immediate situation. All does not stop around you while you write down what you are witnessing. If you find yourself in an educational crisis where things are not going smoothly, students are acting up and your lesson is a shambles, you must first handle the immediate situation. One course of action is to change or leave the activity as gracefully as possible. This will allow you to retain control over the group. However, as we stated in the previous chapter, changing activities must be done carefully so as not to cause more problems for you. Have something "in the wings" to help you get through this troublesome period. Your honesty, showing your students that you recognize that the particular activity is bogging down and you want to improve it or bring in additional materials before going further, will be respected by them. The students, for the most part, know you are not infallible, and they will appreciate that you are willing to acknowledge your mistakes.

Care must be taken, however, to avoid making a practice of changing activities when things start to fail. It is important that you do not allow the class to feel that if they act up you will go to something else that is more fun. Your students may take advantage of this. Remember, that although you may learn as much from your students as they do from you, the teacher should be the primary change agent, not the students. If you have specific objectives that you are working to achieve, try to refrain from straying off target too often. Although exciting discussions and learning situations may grow out of accidental sidetracks, such sidetracks should not be allowed to dominate class time. Has there ever been a class that has not tried drawing their teacher into a conversation about something the teacher is interested in to avoid a less interesting grammar or math assignment or quiz? Allowing yourself to be drawn away from your own objectives may accomplish your students' objectives at the cost of your own program. In this instance, the student objective is to consume your time. This is another instance of the time–snatching behavior discussed in Chapter 5. As you assess your disciplinary structure, you will find that such time–snatching behavior is often going to be the focus of your behavioral records.

Behavioral records may take a number of forms. Despite the variety of records, their purpose is the same, to provide a clear picture of how a student or group of students is behaving in your classroom. One of the clearest pictures is provided by a video tape of your classroom proceedings. A picture *is* worth a thousand words, especially when the picture is of actual classroom behavior. Due to the expense of the equipment involved, video taping devices may be reserved for special projects in most school districts. However, in some, teachers are allowed to use them to tape classroom activities. Many times such equipment sits around not being used because the teachers forget about it or feel that they do not have reason enough to request usage. Using video tapes to improve your teaching effectiveness and your students' behavior is definitely justifiable. If you have access to such equipment, you are fortunate. Such tapes provide a means for observing your students' behavior that will allow you to study at your leisure, removed from the possible turmoil of the moment, who is doing what. The objective eye of the camera may expose potential problem areas that you have not had the time or opportunity to notice. By viewing such tapes both students and teachers can see in black and white where their behavior could be changed so they could become more effective participants in the classroom learning/discipline structure. For this method of observation to be completely successful, you will have to get your students used to the idea that they are being filmed or they are likely "to go Hollywood" on you and their behavior will be unnatural. Thus, you may need to use such equipment for a period of time to let the novelty of it wear off before expecting it to show you true student behavior.

If video tape equipment is unavailable to you or would make you feel uncomfortable, then you must find other ways of recording behavior that are more suitable to your situation. This does not present too much of a problem because a number of economical and easily obtained devices can be used to assist you in recording classroom behavior. A golf counter, a grocery store price counter, as well as behavior counters which are specifically sold for this purpose, can be used easily and effectively to count target behaviors as they occur in your classroom. The golf or behavioral counter pictured in Figure 6.1 will count up to 999 items and is worn like a wristwatch. As a behavior occurs, the teacher pushes the button (stem) on the side and the number is shown in one of the windows. This counter allows you to keep track of target behavior without having to stop what you are doing, find a pencil and the chart and make the appropriate mark.

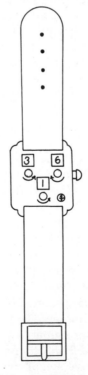

Figure 6.1   Behavior Counter

This device is most effectively used when counting behavior of one specific type (e.g., students talking out of turn) or of one specific person (either yourself or a student). Since it can be quickly reset to zero, you can change from counting one behavior to another with very little time loss.

Discretely used, counting with such a device need not be noticeable to your students since it emits only a quiet click. If your students do notice the counter, however, all is not lost. As a matter of fact, this may be turned to your advantage. We have had classes of students who, when they became aware that the teacher was counting inappropriate behavior, voluntarily improved. Disruptive behavior decreased because no one wanted to be the one caught (or counted). In this instance, that quiet little click was almost as effective as Harry Flotz' revolver.

How long do you observe problem behavior before taking steps to correct it? The answer to this question will depend in part upon what type of misbehavior confronts you. Obviously, serious behavior, such as fighting or drug abuse, which may result in students doing harm to themselves or others, must be dealt with immediately and appropriately. However, less dangerous behavior, which is not necessarily less important in terms of potential damage it might do to the classroom program, may be better dealt with if you do not immediately try to design strategies for dealing with it. For something such as the time–snatching behavior of talking out of turn, a better approach would be to observe and record such behavior for at least five days before setting strategies into effect for dealing with this problem. Using a chart of baseline behavior such as is pictured in Figure 6.2, will show you exactly what level of behavior is operating in the classroom.

The first six days of observation constitute the baseline period wherein the teacher just watched to see how often the behavior occurred.

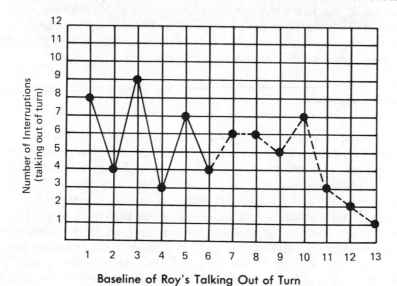

Baseline of Roy's Talking Out of Turn

Figure 6.2

The teacher then put a program into effect of tuning out (ignoring) all statements made by this student before permission had been granted. The broken lines (•--•) on the chart indicate how the student's behavior was affected by this strategy. Although such graphing does take time, it is advantageous in terms of telling you exactly what effect your strategies have upon your student's behavior. You do not have to guess if your program is effective because with such a procedure you will know if, and when your strategy is working. This evaluative phase of anticipative action will be crucial to the success of your total instructional disciplinary structure.

Whatever type of record you choose to make should be further adapted to fit your needs in order to achieve maximum convenience. The simplest form may be a classroom seating chart if your students sit in the same seats each day. This can be made in advance and be easily referred to while your class is in session. Whenever a target behavior occurs you make a check or a dot in the appropriate box. If you do this for one week and record it on a graph, you should have a fairly good idea of how your students' behavior varies from day to day.

Behavior problems do not always have to stem from negative behavior. Having a student in class who tends to monopolize class discussions or answers all the questions can be viewed as a positive behavior problem. Such behavior may squelch the rest of the class and cause them to misbehave or talk out of turn to gain attention. To show this or other behavior you may want to use plusses and minuses on your behavior chart instead of dots or checks. The results of your weekly record may surprise you. They will help you to become much more aware of the scope of the behavior patterns, as well as to identify exactly which individuals are involved in those patterns. Once you have determined which behavior patterns or persons are at the heart of your disciplinary difficulties, you are ready to take action. You can then design strategies that will help make your instructional program more successful to prevent problems and your classroom more pleasant for you and for your students.

Strategies for Controlling Misbehavior

Many differing strategies may be used when trying to control student misbehavior. The primary task to be undertaken when determining which techniques are most effective for your class is to decide which allows you to be successful and still makes you feel most comfortable. It is hard, maybe impossible, to be consistent with any system if you do not really believe in it. Your students will also be more responsive to a program or philosophy if you seem to wholeheartedly support it. As a successful teacher, you must try different models, or different systems of methodology, within your specific classroom, and then choose the one(s) that work(s) best for you. Perhaps an ecclectic model will best serve you and your students' needs. We feel that two methods, the Premack Principle and contracting in contingency management, will further enhance whatever system you select to use within your classroom. The effective employment of such principles can be particularly useful in trying to discourage specific problem behaviors such as were defined earlier.

Premack Principle of High Probability/Low Probability Behavior

---

The Premack Principle states that "behavior normally occurring at a low rate may increase in frequency when it is followed by activities which are highly desirable to the child."[1] In other words, a student is more likely to want to play than to do academic work. Playing is the high-probability behavior (HPB), while academic work is the low-probability behavior (LPB). Thus, telling your students that they will be able to play (or engage in a desired activity) after they have completed their work will increase the likelihood of their doing the work. Obviously, desired activities will differ with age groups and interest levels as well as among individuals of any given group. Enjoyable activities may include such things as free play, working with puzzles, reading books or magazines, listening to records, making bulletin boards or serving as class monitor. An interest assessment done at the beginning of the school term will tell you what the individuals in your class are interested in or would like to do. As was mentioned in Chapter 3, allowing students who have finished their work to do some "fun activity" in the high-interest area of the class will motivate the remaining students to complete their assignments so they can also participate.

A key point to remember is that these high-interest activities should be determined so by the students, not by the teacher. Although you may not relate to their choice, it is essential for their free time activities to be highly desirable to them if this technique is to work. Naturally, you will have to use your judgment in this matter. Some student interests may not be appropriately brought into the classroom. You may have to screen materials (such as books or records brought from home) or provide activities that they will enjoy without taking too much time away from your overall instructional program. For example, endless games of Monopoly may not be too appropriate. However, if you set a limit on the amount of time that can be spent playing such a game, this activity will be more beneficial. Also, these high-interest activities should not be disruptive to the rest of the class. Students wishing to listen to music should do so either with headphones or a listening post while others are working. Also, materials brought into the class by students must be treated carefully. Loss or de-

---

[1] Frank M. Hewett, *The Emotionally Disturbed Child in the Classroom: A Developmental Strategy for Educating Children with Maladaptive Behavior* (Boston: Allyn and Bacon, Inc., 1974), p. 33.

struction of a prized possession will create additional problems.

Not all teachers can employ this principle effectively. Since you are adding another dimension of activity to your class, you must be enough in control that you do not allow high–interest activities to conflict with classwork or to get out of hand. Care must be taken to see that students do not just rush through assignments turning in papers that are filled with errors so they can join in the desired activity. If you allow them to play in these circumstances, you are rewarding them for doing poor work. Thus, it may be necessary to pair high-interest activities with assignments that can be easily corrected. Slipshod work should be redone, not reinforced.

For the Premack principle to work you must allow all children equal availability to the high–interest activity. The brightest child cannot always be using the toys while the slowest is always working. This is both unfair and self-defeating. When first initiating high–interest activities to your classroom, you should give an assignment that everyone can complete so that everyone has the opportunity to share in the fun and will desire to work harder to get the opportunity to play again. You may increase the likelihood of lower ability students having the opportunity to play by having different expectations for their work than you do others. As was mentioned in Chapter 5, this will work best if the assignments or general program is individualized.

In many classrooms students who complete their assignments before the rest of the class are assigned more work to keep them busy while the teacher works with the slower students. After a while, students are apt to rebel against such a practice and become disruptive. Employing the Premack Principle helps to avoid this situation. Also, instead of students doing whatever they please whenever they please, under the application of the Premack Principle you have established guidelines and are teaching them to work to achieve a desired goal: being able to do something special. To avoid misunderstandings and confrontations over who uses what toy or engages in what activity, we advise you to write down (possibly on the chalkboard) under what conditions students will be allowed to participate in high-interest or free-time activities. In a manner of speaking, you will be making a written agreement, or contract, with your class.

Contingency Management: Using Contracts to Best Advantage

Written contracts are helpful in avoiding misunderstandings and misinterpretations of agreements made between the teacher and students. Written contracts can specifically state the conditions under which students can earn "free time" as well as specifically outlining the expectations the teacher holds for improvement in an individual student's behavior. Verbal agreements are open to interpretation and are only as good as the memories of those involved. Unwritten rules and conditions are more likely to become subjective than those that are specifically stated. Classroom conflicts over who can do what for how long during high–interest activities can be avoided if these concerns are clearly defined in the beginning. Such written definitions are not as likely to be changed by intervening situations and circumstances.

To be successful, contracts have essential rules that must be followed. First, the teacher must make the contract student-oriented. As in the case of the Premack Principle, the students must be able to do activities that they want to do—not just those that the teacher wants them to do. This does not mean that all activities have to be purely fun or non-educational in nature. Many educational games which provide additional reinforcement of classroom curriculum may become class or student favorites. Second, the teacher must clearly state the terms of the contract showing how the student's behavior will be evaluated. The terms should include *all of the following:*

1. A specific definition of the high-interest activity that will be earned (e.g., listening to records, reading magazines, etc.)

2. A clear statement of what the student has to do in order to participate in the high-interest activity (e.g., complete the assignment with at least 80% accuracy; or remember to do homework for one week.)

3. A statement of the amount of time that can be spent doing the high-interest activity (e.g., for 10 minutes; until the end of the period; or until the high-interest game is finished, etc.)

The contract will be most successful if it is written in the student's own language with all of the terms explicitly stated.

Above all, the teacher must be careful not to make any commitment that he or she will not be able to fulfill. The idea of the contract is to systematically and fairly reward your students for appropriate behavioral performance, either academic or social. Nothing is to be gained by making a contract that is impossible for either the students or you to fulfill. Agreeing to your students' clamoring for a special activity that is beyond your means or facilities to provide will only weaken your students' trust in you and diminish the effectiveness of contracting as a motivator if you are unable to fulfill your obligation. Purposefully setting up a contract that you feel your students will be unable to complete to avoid paying a desired, but impossible, reward is also a bad practice. To begin with, never underestimate the power of motivation. Your students may surprise you by accomplishing the impossible and expect you to reward them with the impossible in turn. When teaching, making a threat or promise that you cannot fulfill will only reduce your credibility and possibly lead to further student misbehavior.

Contracts for Individuals vs. Contracts for the Entire Class

Up to this point, we have been discussing contracts written for and agreed to by the whole class. However, there are a number of reasons why you may choose to write individual contracts with individual students instead. If you are concerned with individual student behavior, rather than that of the group, you may want to write an individual contract aimed at helping one student behave in a specified way. For example, if John constantly talks to his neighbor or Maria habitually forgets to do her homework, you may want to write individual contracts aimed at improving such behavior. Having mimeographed contract forms ready will allow you to quickly write out contracts that will fit individual needs. One such form to be used with older students is illustrated in Figure 6.3.

```
I,_____, hereby declare that I will
     (student's name)

_____
     (statement of what student has to do)

_____

_____

This job will be considered successfully completed when

_____
     (statement of expected level of proficiency or

_____
     quality of performance)

_____    _____
     Date Signed                    Student Signature

By successfully completing the above activity you may

_____
               (statement of reward)

_____    _____
     Date Completed                 Teacher Signature
```

Figure 6.3   **Sample Written Contract**

```
┌─────────────────────────────────────────────────────────────────┐
│                    "LET'S MAKE A DEAL"                            │
│                                                                   │
│   Contestant:_____       │
│                     (student's name)                             │
│                                                                   │
│                                                                   │
│   Promises to trade_____       │
│                    (statement of what the student has to do)     │
│                                                                   │
│                                                                   │
│   _____       │
│                                                                   │
│                                                                   │
│   _____       │
│                                                                   │
│                                                                   │
│   _____      _____         │
│    Date Promised                Student Signature                │
│                                                                   │
│   For the Big Deal of the Day:_____        │
│                                                                   │
│                                                                   │
│   _____       │
│                                                                   │
│                                                                   │
│   _____       │
│                                                                   │
│                                 Sponsor:_____         │
│   _____                                        │
│         Date Won                                                  │
│                                                                   │
└─────────────────────────────────────────────────────────────────┘
```

Sample Written Contract   **Figure 6.4**

For younger students, you may want to design a contract that is less formalized but equally clear. The contract in Figure 6.4, modeled after the television show, "Let's Make A Deal," would be a more colorful and youthful contract.

Contract forms can be as varied as your students' interest and your creativity allow. A very simple form of contract is the assigning of point value to student work and positive social behavior with the agreement that when a specified number of points are accumulated, the students will be allowed to participate in a high–interest activity.

Making individual contracts may also be necessary to cover possible exceptions to the group's rules. They might be used with students who vehemently disagree with the terms of the group's contract and will not abide by them or students who may not have the necessary skills to successfully complete the terms of the group's contract. Caution should be taken, though, if individual contracts are written for the students of either of these groups. You must be careful not to draw undue attention to or reinforce their inability to conform to group standards. The merits of individual and group contracts should be weighed. Your consideration of your students' individual attitudes, needs, and abilities will help you to decide which approach will be more expedient.

Positive Contracting and
the Effect of the Rules of Reinforcement Theory

Since contracting deals with rewards for appropriate behavior, the rules of reinforcement theory should be followed carefully if the contract program is to be successful. We have previously stated that the contract must be student-oriented, that is, that the students, not just the teacher, believe the reward to be desirable. This is tested by the principle of defining a reward by experience. The only way to determine if the reward is desirable is to check if the appropriate target behavior becomes more frequent after a reward for such behavior has been determined. If your high-interest activity does not encourage appropriate behavior, you may need to reassess the effectiveness of the high-interest activity as a reinforcer. The object of your reinforcement program, the target or inappropriate behavior, should not be too sweeping because behavior is best changed a little bit at a time. Careful sequencing of small amounts of behavioral improvement will in turn lead to the accomplishment of the broader goal. Avoiding expecting too much of your students at one time results in less pressure and a more enjoyable educational environment for all involved.

The efficacy of immediate reward is also an important rule to remember. When something is first being learned, learning will progress best if every instance of the desired behavior is reinforced. This principle of extinction (the fact that if no reward follows behavior, the behavior will extinguish or become less frequent) is exceedingly important when dealing with inappropriate behavior. Not all teachers are aware that they unwittingly reinforce their students' inappropriate behavior through their facial expressions or tone of voice. When dealing with negative or inappropriate behavior, it is important to remember that an intermittent schedule of reinforcement (i.e., rewarding inconsistently) is stronger than a fixed ration (rewarding every time). Very few people will smile every time a student acts out or disrupts the class, but that occasional smile at the wrong time can prolong the students' inappropriate behavior patterns.

One goal of teaching is for students to establish voluntarily controlled behavior, that is, for the students to behave appropriately without being specifically rewarded every time by the teacher. Students will control their own behavior voluntarily for a variety of reasons. The motivation may stem from their own feelings of accomplishment, a desire for social acceptance, or a desire to avoid arguments or hassles. Reaching this point of voluntarily controlled behavior is accomplished after careful movement away from a fixed schedule of reinforcement to a more intermittent one. Care must be taken, however, to proceed gradually because too abrupt a change from continuous to intermittent reinforcement may cause the desired behavior to cease. Knowing which behavior or levels of performance to reward or ignore (the principle of selective rewards) is a key element in helping your students to behave appropriately in the classroom

Constructing a positive teacher-controlled classroom is dependent upon the teacher's awareness of the effects of all behavior, both the teacher's and the students', within the classroom. Understanding what constitutes inappropriate behavior within the confines of your program and school environment is most important. Determining which strategies for dealing with student misbehavior is both in keeping with your general philosophy of teaching and your movement toward the attainment of an educational atmosphere that is most conducive to learning is one of the most complicated tasks that face the teacher. We do not offer the techniques mentioned within this chapter as total solutions for classroom behavioral problems. However, we do feel that such techniques may become valuable tools when integrated with your own philosophy in the total educational program of your classroom.

The following Summary of Behavioral Analysis is a 10-step assessment tool adapted by the Superintendent of Schools, Department of Education, San Diego County, California, in 1975 for usage in an EHA, Title IV-B Project developed under ESEA, Title III. It is included in *Teaching Interpersonal Social Skills: a manual of activities for teachers of educationally handicapped children.* Such an analysis uses the information and techniques that were outlined in the previous chapter. Choose the behavior of one of your students that you feel seriously interferes with classroom learning and analyze it in this manner.

A SUMMARY OF BEHAVIOR ANALYSIS

Adapted from a Title IV-B Workshop
By Dwight S. Goodwin
California State University, San Jose

Step 1　　Describe the *undesirable* behavior.

_____

_____

_____

_____

Next, estimate how often the undesirable behavior occurs. (Check appropriate box.)

　　a. Once a day　　　　　　　　　☐

　　b. Two to ten times a day　　☐

　　c. More than ten times a day　☐

Step 2　　Describe the behavior you would like to take the place of the *undesirable* behavior.

_____

_____

_____

_____

Finally, describe any behavior that the student already possesses that might help achieve the desired behavior.

_____

_____

_____

_____

Try to estimate how often these last behaviors occur each day. (Check appropriate box.)

a. Once a day ☐

b. Two to five times a day ☐

c. Six to ten times a day ☐

d. More than ten times a day ☐

Copy the undesirable behavior from Step 1 here.   **Step 3**

_____

_____

Describe what happens before the *undesirable* behavior occurs.

What is the curriculum?

a. Subject matter and activity
   (math, P.E., writing, listening)   _____

b. Length of time for assignment   _____

c. Accuracy required for
   assignment   _____

d. How presented (e.g., writ-
   ten/verbal directions)   _____

e. Physical environment (e.g., inside, outside, in corner, etc.)   _____

f. Other   _____

What is the social context of the undesirable behavior? (Check appropriate boxes.)

Teacher leads/participates		*Teacher doesn't lead/participate*	
a. Individual	☐	a. Individual	☐
b. Small group	☐	b. Small group	☐
c. Class	☐	c. Class	☐

What else in the environment might trigger this behavior?

_____

_____

_____

Copy the undesirable behavior from Step 1 here.   **Step 4**

_____

_____

Describe what happens afterwards.

When this behavior happens, what does/do

The teacher does

	frequently	sometimes	seldom
a. _____	_____	_____	_____
b. _____	_____	_____	_____

The peers do

	frequently	sometimes	seldom
a. _____	_____	_____	_____
b. _____	_____	_____	_____

Others do

	frequently	sometimes	seldom
a. _____	_____	_____	_____
b. _____	_____	_____	_____

What is the effect on the pupil's work?

	frequently	sometimes	seldom
a. Doesn't begin	_____	_____	_____
b. Doesn't participate.	_____	_____	_____
c. Doesn't complete.	_____	_____	_____
d. Doesn't turn in assignment.	_____	_____	_____

What else follows the undesirable behavior?

	frequently	sometimes	seldom
a. _____	_____	_____	_____
b. _____	_____	_____	_____

Step 5   Copy the desired behavior from Step 2 here.

_____

_____

Describe what happens before the *desired* behavior occurs

What is the curriculum?

a. Activity (e.g., writing, listening, etc.   _____

b. Length of time for assignment   _____

c. Accuracy required for assignment
_____

d. How presented (e.g., written/verbal directions)
_____

e. Physical environment (e.g., inside, outside, etc.)
_____

f. Other
_____

What is the social context when the desirable behavior occurs? (Check appropriate boxes.)

Teacher leads/participates		*Teacher doesn't lead/participate*	
a. Individual	☐	a. Individual	☐
b. Small group	☐	b. Small group	☐
c. Class	☐	c. Class	☐

What else in the environment might trigger the desired behavior?
_____
_____

Copy the desired behavior from Step 2 here.
_____
_____

Step 6

Describe what happens afterwards.

When this behavior happens, what does/do

The teacher does

	frequently	sometimes	seldom
a. _____	_____	_____	_____
b. _____	_____	_____	_____

The peers do

	frequently	sometimes	seldom
a. _____	_____	_____	_____
b. _____	_____	_____	_____

Others do
(*nurse, principal, parent, etc.*)

	frequently	sometimes	seldom
a. _____	_____	_____	_____
b. _____	_____	_____	_____

What is the effect on the pupil's work?

	frequently	sometimes	seldom
a. Does begin	_____	_____	_____
b. Does participate.	_____	_____	_____
c. Does complete.	_____	_____	_____
d. Does turn in assignment.	_____	_____	_____

What else follows the desired behavior?

	frequently	sometimes	seldom
a. _____	_____	_____	_____
b. _____	_____	_____	_____

Step 7　Increasing the *desired* behavior

Curriculum—What changes can be made to increase the likelihood that the desired behavior will occur?

a. Subject matter and activity (math, reading, listening, etc.) _____

b. Length of time for assignment _____

c. Accuracy required for assignment _____

d. Manner of presentation (e.g., oral/written directions) _____

e. Physical environment (e.g., inside, outside, in corner, etc.) _____

f. Other _____

Social context—What changes could be made in the social context to increase the likelihood that the desired behavior will occur?

a. What condition should be set? _____

b. Should the pupil be working with someone? _____

c. What are the conditions under which this is possible? _____

d. For how long? _____

What explanations (if any) should be given beforehand?

    a. The amount of work to be
       performed?   _____

    b. The amount of time to com-
       plete work?   _____

Increasing the *desired* behavior: **Step 8**

What does the student do when he has finished as a signal that he has completed his task?

_____

_____

_____

How is the task to be checked for accuracy, etc.?

_____

_____

_____

What is the arrangement for payoff? (immediate, delayed, schedule)

_____

_____

_____

What options can students select for types of rewards and/or when they are delivered?

_____

_____

_____

Copy the undesirable behavior from Step 1 here.   **Step 9**

_____

_____

Alternatives for *undesirable* behavior:

What consequences do you plan to use if the undesirable behavior occurs?

_____

_____

_____

Explain the consequences if the undesirable behavior occurs.

_____

_____

Describe what can be used as a signal to the student if the undesirable behavior occurs.

_____
_____
_____

Describe what the student is to do or where he is to go when he sees or hears the signal.

_____
_____
_____

Step 10   Copy the undesirable behavior from Step 1 here.

_____
_____

Decreasing the *undesirable* behavior:

Describe the consequences that are to follow when the undesirable behavior occurs (those you and/or the student have decided upon).

a. _____

b. _____

c. _____

d. _____

Note: Be sure to state these conditions so that everyone agrees on what they are . . . . be specific!

Foster, Carol, *Developing Self-Control*. Kalamazoo, Michigan: Behavior-delia, Inc., 1974.

Hall, R. Vance, *Managing Behavior 1—Behavior Modification: The Measurement of Behavior*. Lawrence, Kansas: H & H Enterprises, Inc., 1971.

Hewett, Frank M., *The Emotionally Disturbed Child in the Classroom. A developmental strategy for educating children with maladaptive behavior*. Boston: Allyn and Bacon, Inc., 1974.

Holland, James G., and B. F. Skinner, *The Analysis of Behavior*. New York: McGraw-Hill, 1961.

Leitenberg, Harold, ed., *Handbook of Behavior Modification and Behavior Therapy*. Englewood Cliffs, N.J.: Prentice-Hall, Inc., 1976.

Morris, Richard J., *Behavior Modification with Children: a systematic guide*. Cambridge, Massachusetts: Winthrop Publishers, Inc., 1976.

Wike, Edward L., *Secondary Reinforcement: selected experiments*. New York: Harper & Row, 1966.

"Discipline: Its central relationship to subject matter teaching," *Professional Growth for Teachers*, 9, No. 1 (1963), p. 1.

7 Improving Classroom Communication

What most people think of as discipline is ineptly delivered discipline. That is the raising of the voice, threatening, sending a kid to the principal's office. When it's done effectively, discipline is almost invisible, so low-key and so precise, just moment to moment, that it prevents rather than terminates the majority of disruptions.

Frederic H. Jones

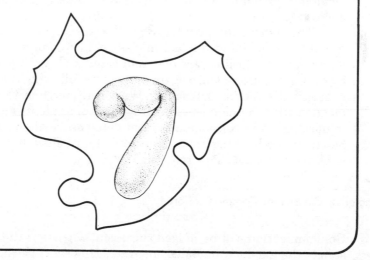

Communicate: to give, or give and recieve, information, signals, or messages in any way, as by talk, gestures, writing, etc.[1]

Communication is such an encompassing process that it filters through all human activities. No living person is unaffected by communication. Learning is, at heart, the expression of communication. Learning correct information in an appropriate fashion is dependent upon both the effective sending and receiving of the information. Two types of communication pervade the classroom environment. In the first, working in a strictly verbal-auditory mode of communication, the teacher is the focus in that he or she gives the information or sends the messages to the students. In the second, there is a duality of participation, an interplay, in which the coordination of efforts by the teacher and students results in learning.

This second type of communication is what we have been discussing throughout this text. The quality and effectiveness of this communication is dependent upon all of the variables of the teaching process that we have discussed up to this point: teacher and student anxieties, the school environment, group dynamics, curriculum management and behavior modification or disciplinary strategies. The effectiveness of each of these variables is, in turn, dependent upon the quality of communication in the classroom.

This two-way communication is a dynamic process in which the teacher and students change postures constantly, sharing the responsibility for sending and receiving messages. The manner in which these messages are sent and received will determine whether your classroom teacher-student relationships are positive or negative, whether learning is facilitated or hampered, or whether discipline tactics are preventive or ineffective.

Throughout this chapter, we will be discussing the aspects that lead to both the good and the bad in classroom communications. We will be discussing how feelings are communicated and how feelings are affected by communications. Once again, we will be following the preventive path of anticipative action in teaching. We will discuss how to improve communication with the requisite understanding of students and modes of communication to be considered in great detail as we discuss how appropriate behavior and learning are reinforced and misbehavior and learning problems are extinguished or reduced.

The Character of Classroom Communication

Communication can be judged successful whenever the recipient understands the sender's intended message. However, because the effects of

---

[1] Joseph H. Friend and David B. Guralnik, eds., *Webster's New World Dictionary of the American Language,* College Edition (Cleveland: World Publishing Company, 1959), p. 296.

such messages upon the participants can be both good and bad, these messages can be characterized as being either positive or negative. Positive classroom communication is that in which understanding is increased or information is transmitted in such a way that the teacher and students learn from each other in a pleasant, workable atmosphere. On the other hand, negative classroom communication is that which conflicts with or thwarts the acquisition of knowledge or understanding of ideas, statements, or feelings of either the teacher or student. This is seen when the teacher tries to say one thing but ends up saying another. Such a situation occurs when the teacher gives classroom directions that no one understands, or tries to discipline a student or student group for misbehavior and is met with student mirth, contempt or apathy. In such situations, further misunderstandings, misinterpretations, frustrations, tensions, and behavioral disorders are generated.

When communication becomes negative, teacher paralysis and over-reaction discussed in Chapter 1 is more likely to occur. This, in turn, leads to time-snatching where too much time is spent with the teacher justifying motives, methods and content while the class slowly goes out of control. How is this disruptive cycle precipitated? Generally, this is done by misperceptions or by negative communication in which the teacher is unable to get across what he or she wants to express.

An example of negative communication occurs wherever students are reluctant to raise their hands and say they do not understand what is going on. If students do not feel comfortable saying, "I don't understand what you said or mean," the instructional activity will plow along losing students by the wayside. Student misbehavior flourishes in such an environment. The teacher's reaction to such misbehavior will also be negative, if instead of trying to positively solve the problem of disinterested or disobedient students, he or she becomes defensive and ridicules or retaliates by squelching student feelings or performance. Discovering the basis of this breakdown in communication can best be accomplished by analyzing the relations of the elements that combine to impede or enhance understanding of messages.

Elements of Communication: Verbal and Nonverbal Messages

Classroom communication, like all other kinds of communication, is comprised of both verbal and nonverbal behavior. These two elements equally influence the quality of communication in the classroom. Employed properly, verbal and nonverbal messages can assist you in effectively teaching and meeting your objectives for particular students or the entire class. Teachers who pay little attention to either the verbal and nonverbal makeup of their messages to their students, or to those of their students' messages to them, may be plagued by miscommunication resulting in reduced performance and success for both teachers and students. To avoid confusion and misunderstandings, teachers should always strive to say exactly what they mean to say. To do this you must always be aware of all facets of verbal and nonverbal communication.

The Influence of Verbal and Nonverbal Messages. Saying exactly what you mean to say is not an easy process, especially if you are already under stress. The first obstacle to overcome when trying to improve clarity in teacher–student messages is inappropriate word usage. The words that you choose will either help clarify your message to your students or mystify them further. To determine the effectiveness of your word choice you can ask yourself the following questions:

1. Do you use words that your students clearly understand or have appropriate connotations for them?

2. When you are praising or encouraging your students, do you always use the same words?

3. Does your syntax facilitate understanding?

If you choose words that are immediately recognizable or understandable to your students or provide adequate information about or a definition of the words you use, you may not have problems in this area. The tricky part comes when you try to decide the connotations that your words will have for your students. This is especially important when you deal with a student or students whose ethnic background differs from your own. If their life experiences and attitudes are in marked contrast to yours, their reactions to words may also vary dramatically from yours. Mistakes in this area are hard to avoid because, in many cases, you do not know you are saying anything wrong until after you have already said it. However, listening carefully to what your students say and mean and learning from your own mistakes will help you in this area.

If you use encouragement or praise to motivate your students to learn or behave better, the words you choose for encouragement or praise will have a major bearing on your ultimate success in this area. Relying on one or two pat phrases will not be as effective as choosing from a variety of expressions to convey your pride, pleasure, or satisfaction with their individual endeavors. If you always say, "You're doing a good job," your words will lose meaning and value for your students. If you are extremely limited in your use of social reinforcers (e.g., set smiles or hackneyed expressions of encouragement) your students are not as likely to be as motivated as you would like. Table 7.1 lists examples of a variety of words and phrases that could be substituted for old standbys for encouragement and praise.

We also feel that you should draw from your own wealth of personal expressions that may border on slang but which will convey your feelings very sincerely to your students. Different generations, even decades, have greatly differing ways of expressing the same thing: "That is good," or "I like that." Although your students may not be immediately able to relate to such personalized expressions, as, "that's the cat's pajamas" or "that's neat," they can clearly tell from your enthusiasm that you are happy about them or their work because of your sincere manner and words. They may pick up some of your expressions and you will undoubtedly pick up some of theirs as you relate and communicate together.

Examples of Encouragement and Praise   Table 7.1

Encouragers

"I'm pleased with what you're doing!"
"You're really working hard, aren't you?"
"I know you will finish on time."
"You're really paying attention today."
"This is really going to be beautiful!"

Praise

"Wow! That's super!"
"Great!"
"Outstanding!"
"Excellent work!"
"Good idea!"
"Fine job!"
"You really tried hard, didn't you!"
"That was a nice thing to do!"
"How helpful!"
"You are really cooperating today!"
"I'm happy with you!"
"I like that!"
"Very interesting."
"Now, that was smart!"
"You thought of that all by yourself—how original!"
"Good thinking!"

Your syntax is a crucial element in your communicating with students. As we have mentioned previously, the way you give instructions, ask questions or state explanations must be very clear if your students are to effectively participate or learn in your classroom. Your instructions should be sequenced. By this, we mean you should carefully consider the proper order and amount of things that you ask your students to do in a given activity. If you string too many directions together you are likely to lose the students who do not have great memories. For example, problems will occur if you quickly say, "Students, sit down, get your social studies book out and turn to page 306. Be sure you use a pencil and lined paper when answering questions 1 to 12." In those two sentences, the teacher asked the students to do seven things. This might be difficult for many students, but it would be impossible for younger students or those who can remember no more than two or three things at a time. Breaking down these directions in smaller units or pausing to allow the students to complete one action before plunging ahead with more directions will help alleviate confusion and instructional problems.

While analyzing the effects that your word usage may have upon your intended meaning, you must also determine how characteristics of your voice might be affecting your message clarity and overall instructional program. Your vocal volume and inflection will greatly affect the successful reception of your intended messages. Your meaning, emphasis, and many times, the amount of influence you have with your students, will be communicated by these language components.

The primary thing to determine when considering voice level is whether you speak loudly enough for everyone to hear during the general flow of activity in your classroom. This is not best determined either by repeatedly asking the group whether they can hear you or by constantly increasing your volume whenever there is a lot of conflicting chatter or noise in the room. Either of these responses can cause more problems in terms of increased student disruptions. Some students enjoy seeing how much they can make their teachers yell at them. This is an energy-wasting power struggle in which each side tries to see which will be able to out-yell the other. (When it is 30 to 1, the odds are not in the teacher's favor.) Any teacher who is constantly close to shouting will not be able to increase his or her vocal volume if and when it is needed for emphasis or control. You have to decide whether the students are experiencing difficulties with understanding, hearing, or attending to you because of your own communication problems or their behavioral problems (or a combination of the two).

If you always speak at the same volume and your students easily hear you and follow along through fun activities but cannot hear you clearly during less popular activities, you know you are not dealing with speech and hearing problems. In such a situation, your students are doing selective listening (i.e., hearing only those things they want to hear). You must deal with this behavior as you would with any other disruptive behavior. First, you identify the circumstances in which this problem arises and exactly who is involved in this situation. You can then determine strategies to help you in working with them to change this interfering behavior. This can be accomplished possibly by choosing one or several of the following strategies:

1. Moving students who have difficulty hearing in the back closer to the front

2. Managing the social climate through knowledge of group dynamics

3. Individual contracting or reinforcement of appropriate behavior

4. Discussing the problem with the student or students involved

Whatever method you choose to use will be dependent on your own teaching style and your students' needs and personalities. Whether these strategies will be solutions to this problem will be demonstrated when you assess the effects of these strategies upon the operation of your classroom. The evaluative method can be as simple as noticing a decrease in the number of "I can't hear you's" or as complicated as recording inappropriate behavior to see the extent and duration of the change.

Your tone of voice also conveys meaning to your students. Your vocal modulation and tone serve as major cues to your students. From them, they will determine whether you are serious about what you are saying, and even whether you are secure and in command of the general situation. Students do not question the teacher's authority, if the teacher confidently and honestly presents his or her knowledge, programs, standards and self image. They may not like aspects of these things, but they will not question the authority involved if the teacher is confident in his or her abilities and position.

Thus, confidence in yourself and your abilities is the starting point in your resolution of instructional and disciplinary difficulties. If your voice quavers when you speak to your class, your students are much more likely to doubt your abilities to lead them. If *you* do not lead them, students will rise to the task and student leadership will not always be in the interest of good learning if students' objectives and methods conflict with those of your educational program. If, on the other hand, you speak in a calm and self-assured way, your vocal qualities will assist you in directing activities and students.

This does not mean to say that you have to be so low-key that you never let your excitement and enthusiasm for students and activities show. If you believe in what you are doing, and truly are excited or interested in an activity, your students will be much more likely to participate fully and voluntarily in the activity. This is especially true when you first introduce an activity, procedure or unit. Students will become enthusiastic if you are enthusiastic, or they will quickly become apathetic or turned off if you act as though you already know they will not like it before they even start. This is another example of a self-fulfilling prophecy. If you can speak positively and exuberantly, you and your ideas will be much more likely to be accepted by your students.

Since teachers are not automatons, they will experience a wide gamut of feelings throughout their dealings and relationships with students. Your students will undoubtedly do things that will anger or upset you. They need to know which things are inappropriate. They need to know that you do not like or tolerate certain behavior; and at the same time they need to know that your dislike is *for a specific behavior* that they are in control of—*not dislike for them as persons.* The honest expression of your feelings in an appropriate manner will help you to build rapport with and to improve communications with them. An open, human, and humane environment is essential for establishing two-way communication with your students.

Although your words and voice are the prime communicators of meaning to your students, nonverbal aspects of your messages are equally as important. Their effects must be considered when you are assessing where your classroom communication needs improvement. Eye contact, body space (i.e., your proximity to another person when you are talking to them), your posture, gestures and facial expressions will either contribute to or hamper your communications and disciplinary actions. A teacher who slouches under stress, has poor eye contact, or is reluctant to get close to students, is not as likely to command the students' respect as is the teacher who can look disruptive students straight in the eye and move comfortably and self-assuredly whether dealing with disturbances or instructing.

Your body language constantly communicates meaning to your students. Care must be taken that such nonverbal messages do not conflict with your verbal messages. Such a process, in which double or conflicting messages are sent to your students, must be curtailed if you want to effectively communicate with your students. You can communicate double messages in the following ways:

1. Laughing while you are speaking of a serious situation (this is not as ridiculous as it sounds because many people laugh or giggle when they are nervous)

2. Frowning while you are telling students they are doing well

3. Always standing behind a podium or sitting behind a table or desk while instructing

4. Leaning away from your students while saying you want to get to know them

5. Impatiently tapping your fingers while you help a slower student try to catch up with the rest of the class

To avoid confusing your students in such ways, you must be aware of how you look and act as well as what you say while communicating, disciplining, and instructing.

Determining Meaning in Student–Teacher Communications

Having the students clearly understand all the teacher's messages is a major instructional communication goal. Student confusion about meaning can be reduced if you choose words that are both specific and relevant to their level of experience. Carefully choosing your words can avoid the problem presented in *The Family Circus* cartoon.

Often the meaning you intend for your words to convey is not the meaning that your listeners choose to hear or understand. Thus, care must be taken to specify the exact outcome that you expect when you give directions. This is especially true if you have a particularly literal student

THE FAMILY CIRCUS   by Bil Keane

"But, a little while ago you said you weren't gonna ask me to clean up my room again."

who follows directions to the letter, such as by taking all of the books and supplies out and sitting inside his desk when directed, "Roy, sit in your desk." Obviously, saying precisely what you mean could have prevented this problem. For example, you might have been better off saying, "Roy, return to your assigned seat and sit down." With such a student, you may have difficulty specifying everything to the degree that is necessary to avoid such behavior.

Carefully thinking before you speak will more effectively reduce disruptions than arguing with the student about certain behavior after it has already occurred. When a student takes advantage of a slip of your tongue, you must take great pains not to reinforce this behavior by giving it undue attention or the behavior will be likely to recur. In such a circumstance, smiling at a student's antics when you are displeased with the behavior is an example of sending an inconsistent double message and should be avoided. If careful word selection and appropriate response do not eliminate such behavior, you may wish to use some other means, such as contracting to extinguish this persistent disruption.

When trying to solve problems in class social interactions with your students, you must discuss problems in the clearest manner possible. To avoid further conflict and confusion, you must use and define common terms in a way that is understandable and acceptable to all. This will be fundamental in your students' discussing, understanding, and positively dealing with problem behavior.

One program, designed for the Omaha public school system in 1973 by Positive Peer Culture, Inc. (PPC), was aimed at maximizing such communication. The program's goals were to increase the students' understanding of themselves and to decrease fighting, vandalism, and defiance toward authority figures while training students to become leaders who would help peers to become academically, emotionally, and socially successful in school. This was accomplished in part by defining common terms, so that student problems could be discussed more effectively, and limiting the interpretation of student behavior. The program identified twelve types of behavioral problems which were described in peer language, a partial list of which follows.

Positive Peer Culture—Description of Problems

1. *Low self-image: has a poor opinion of self; often feels put down or of little worth.*

   a. Feels unlucky; a loser, rejected, mistreated; feels sorry for himself (herself); has no confidence (s)he can be of value to others.
   b. Worries that something is wrong with him (her), feels inadequate, thinks (s)he is good for nothing, is afraid others will find out "how bad I really am . . ."

2. *Inconsiderate of others: does things that are damaging to others.*

   a. Does things that hurt people, enjoys putting people down.
   b. Acts selfishly, doesn't care about the needs or feelings of others.

3. *Inconsiderate of self: does things that are damaging to self.*

   a. Puts self down, brings anger and ridicule on self, does things that hurt self.
   b. Acts as though (s)he doesn't want to improve self or solve problems.

4. *Authority problem: does not want to be managed by anyone.*

   a. Views authority as an enemy camp "out to get him (her)."
   b. Resents anybody's telling him (her) what to do; does not readily accept advice from either adults or peers.

5. *Misleads others: draws others into negative behavior.*

   a. Seeks status by being a negative or delinquent leader.
   b. Gives support to the negative or delinquent actions of others.

156

6. *Easily misled: is drawn into negative behavior by others.*

   a. Can't make his (her) own decisions and is easily controlled by stronger persons.
   b. Can't stand up for what (s)he believes, even when (s)he knows (s)he is right.

7. *Aggravates others: treats people in negative hostile ways.*

   a. Makes fun of others; tries to embarrass them and make them feel low.
   b. Seeks attention in negative ways; irritates or annoys people.
   c. Makes subtle threats in word or manner.

8. *Easily angered; is often irritated or provoked, or has tantrums.*

   a. Frequently becomes upset or explosive, but may try to excuse such behavior as naturally "having a bad temper."
   b. Easily frustrated; unable to accept failure or disappointments.

9. *Stealing: takes things that belong to others.*

   a. Thinks it is all right to steal if you are sneaky enough not to get caught.
   b. Doesn't respect others and is willing to hurt another person to get what (s)he wants.

10. *Alcohol or drug problems: misuses substances that could hurt self.*

    a. Afraid (s)he won't have friends if (s)he doesn't join with them in drugs or drinking.
    b. Thinks drugs are cool; tries to impress others with his (her) drug knowledge or experience.

11. *Lying: cannot be trusted to tell the truth.*

    a. Tells stories because (s)he thinks others will like him (her) better.
    b. Likes to live in a make-believe fantasy world.

12. *Fronting: puts on an act rather than being real.*

    a. Needs to appear big in the eyes of others; always needs to try to prove him (her) self.
    b. Bluffs and cons people; thinks loudness and slick talk are better than reason.[2]

The success of such a program demonstrates the value of one method which attempts to improve teachers' communications with stu-

---

[2] "Positive Peer Culture: a system based on Tender Loving Care," *Creative Discipline: Searching for the better way*, 1, No. 3 (November, 1977–January, 1978), pp. 5–6.

"WHAT **YOU** CALL 'STANDIN' UP FOR MY RIGHTS', **SHE** CALLS 'SASSIN' BACK'!" *

dents and students' communication with authority figures, as well as peers. The meanings of experiences and words were carefully analyzed to help them learn about and improve themselves. Learning to relate on a neutral level where feelings and experiences are openly discussed and understood is the first step in a program of positive communication. When both sides try to understand each other's meanings or perceptions of behavior and their consequences, confusions such as the one portrayed in the *Dennis the Menace* cartoon can be avoided.

Improving Communication While Discouraging Student Misbehavior

Your understanding of the relationship between the elements that make up your communications with your students can help you to improve upon the clarity of your messages and their messages. This is generally

---

* *DENNIS THE MENACE* ® cartoon © by Field Enterprises, Inc.

the primary communication concern of teachers. Another area which is equally important is how all of these elements of language can be used to reinforce your students' appropriate behavior and extinguish misbehavior. These language-based disciplinary strategies are accomplished through such means as social and tangible reinforcement, assertive teaching behavior and your own selective listening.

Providing Positive Feedback Through Social and Tangible Reinforcement

Your students' appropriate behavior will be more likely to occur or recur if you build an atmosphere of warmth and acceptance in which positive behavior is reinforced positively. Typical types of social reinforcers that you can use to help students to feel successful and comfortable in school are:

1. verbal praise

2. opportunities for peer recognition

3. encouragement

4. acknowledgement of the student's presence or entrance into class by words or smiles

5. sending home positive progress reports to parents

6. maintaining eye contact when a student desires your attention

7. maintaining proximity during class activities

8. friendly physical actions such as winks, hugging, hand clasps, pats on the shoulder

9. friendly looks

10. speaking pleasantly (friendly tone)

11. nodding encouragingly

12. applauding good performance

One of the most important reinforcements, not included in this list, is accomplished by just listening to your students, by participating in conversations that are enjoyable to them, and by allowing them to discuss things they are interested in. Such actions let your students know that you value them as people and give them clear-cut feedback of what behavior you deem appropriate in the classroom. Students like to feel good about themselves (as we all do) and will be responsive to positive statements of their self-worth.

While such social reinforcement is probably a natural component of your dealings with your students, many times teachers may feel their students need a more tangible type of reinforcement to help improve their behavior. Such a program was undertaken by the Arrowhead School in Collegeville, Pennsylvania[3] in order to minimize the disciplinary problems of the student body in a newly-designed open-education program. The students were unused to open space and flexible buildings with no doors, so the staff instituted a school-wide token reinforcement program entitled, "Catch a Child Being Good." In this program, every adult on the staff with daily contact with students, from the cafeteria workers to the principal and custodians, was given the opportunity to recognize and reward positive student behavior and student courtesy by writing up green slips that indicated praiseworthy behavior. The green slips were valuable to the students because when used as money they could buy treats or food at the school store. Also they could be used to earn field trips with the principal or to participate in the school television program. The value of such a program is that the entire focus was on positive or appropriate behaviors. Two-way communication is seen to be working effectively when both school staff and students work together and are concerned with the establishment of a positive and well-disciplined atmosphere.

Effects of Assertive Teacher Behavior upon Student–Teacher Communication

Having the ability to say what you mean to say in such a way that your students understand your meaning and comply with your request for a specific behavior is an important characteristic of a successful classroom teacher. Assertive teaching behavior is aimed at reducing interpersonal anxiety while promoting more open and successful communication in this area. Your mode of requesting behavior from your students will be an important determiner of your success in dealing with their inappropriate behavior. In his book entitled, *Assertive Discipline,*[4] Lee Canter gives examples of four methods of requesting behavior:

1. *Hints*—"Everyone should be working."

2. *Questions*—"Would you please get to work?"

3. *"I" messages*—"I want you to open your books and get to work."

4. *Demands*—"Get to work now."

Overreliance on demanding behavior, rather than the other three, is a very poor teaching practice. Method 4 uses a threat to get students to do work. If they do not do something you say, something unpleasant will occur. This changes the teacher's posture from a helper to that of an ad-

[3] "Arrowhead School: Where Learning is a Joy," *Creative Discipline: Searching for the better way,* 1, No. 3 (November, 1977–January, 1978), pp. 15–17.

[4] Lee Canter with Marlene Canter, *Assertive Discipline: A Take Charge Approach for Today's Educator* (Seal Beach, Cal.: Canter and Associates, Inc., 1976), p. 72.

versary. This sets the scene for endless behavior problems and power struggles between the class and the teacher.

There is an important difference between being aggressive and being assertive. An adversary is in an aggressive position. When you are aggressive, you may make demands, threats, yell, and become to some degree abusive. On the other hand, the assertive teacher will make clear, calm, controlled and defined statements which do not threaten either the teacher's or students' dignity. Assertion is a means of establishing your authority in the classroom. It allows you to establish this classroom authority more positively than aggression does.

Assertive behavior includes the verbal and nonverbal elements of communication that were discussed earlier in this chapter. When you are assertive, you avoid double messages. Assertive statements of fact do not cause your students to respond as if you are asking a question. Such miscommunication could be due to your words, actions or both. For example, if you are trying to be assertive you should not make the following statements:

"We are going to start working now. OK?"
"You are the team captain, Sue. All right?"

Or displaying the "you know" syndrome, which is characterized by making a statement like the following:

"Heather, it is your turn to start, you know?"

Tacking on these questioning endings changes clear statements into rhetorical questions. You really do not expect an answer but you may receive one and that answer may be in opposition to your direction, thus causing a disruption in your activities.

Your nonverbal behavior can also cause your students to question your meaning and authority. Looking at the back wall or out the window while you are addressing a member of the class or the whole group is nonassertive and will likely cause your students to pay less attention to what you are saying than where you are looking. Such nonassertion (and lack of attention) may result in an unproductive "Who, me?" when you ask class members a question but do not look at them while doing so.

When you want to be assertive, you maintain eye contact with students when appropriate, remembering that cultural and ethnic differences may make eye contact inappropriate in certain situations.[5] You should maintain close proximity to your students, face them and speak clearly in both tone and meaning. Your words and manner will convey both your meaning and your reactions to your students' words and behavior. Teaching assertively is based on your command of the total situation and

---

[5] Sherwin B. Cotler and Julio J. Guerra, *Assertion Training: A humanistic behavioral guide to self-dignity* (Champaign, Ill.: Research Press, 1976), p. 105.

yourself. When you are assertive, anxieties should be reduced and conflicts between you and your students will not be prolonged due to game-playing or confusing message-sending on your part.

Using Selective Listening to Everyone's Advantage

The practice of selective listening (or tuning out) is ignoring students or their behavior when they are seeking your attention in an inappropriate way or at an inappropriate time. The average teacher who teaches a group of 30 students will be constantly besieged by students seeking either attention. For the sake of efficiency and practicality, you cannot pay individual attention to everyone at once. When the students' verbal behavior becomes disruptive, as when a student time-snatcher asks off-the-subject questions or shouts out answers to questions before you can call on someone else, selective listening can be a valuable aid in lessening this behavior. You can deal with both of these problems by addressing only students who follow prescribed procedures or try to stay on task. If the student disrupts the whole class proceedings with inappropriate questions and responses just to get your attention, you should ignore these disruptions. When you do this consistently, your students will soon learn that this strategy for gaining your attention is not working and their disruptive behavior should become less frequent and eventually stop.

Care must be taken not to get caught up in too many "Whodunit" games in which the teacher, in the role of an educational Sherlock Holmes, leaves no stone unturned to find out who whispered a profane word or called him or her a name at recess. Too much attention paid to such behavior will most likely result in an increase in the inappropriate behavior of your students. When practicing selective listening, you teach your students that you will give them your attention when they behave in a manner that is in line with your standards or with established class rules.

Although selective listening is not appropriate in every situation, when you do find it necessary to employ this technique, you are in charge. You must make the choice of which behavior you will deal with directly. There is no reason for you to do battle over every issue, and it is not inconsistent to ignore one behavior that is aimed at gaining your attention while setting up a contract for dealing with another. Your choice should be based on what you determine is beneficial for your student, your class, and your program.

Selective listening should not be confused with appeasement. Rather than giving in to avoid trouble, you are using a specific technique to control a specific behavior with the hope that the behavior will grow less desirable to the student.

Our discussion of communication in this chapter has been limited to that which occurs between the teacher and students in the classroom. In the next chapter, we will extend our discussion to include communications and relations between teachers, the total staff, and parents.

1. Evaluate the verbal and nonverbal elements which generally characterize your communication with the students. How do *you* socially reinforce your students' behavior? How could these be improved to be more effective? **1**

2. What do your students do, verbally and nonverbally, to reinforce your behavior? **2**

3. Would a program such as the Positive Peer Culture program be beneficial for your students? What problem behavior would you think would be most beneficial for your students to discuss? How would you generate student definitions for these problems? **3**

"Arrowhead School: Where learning is a joy," *Creative Discipline: Searching for the better way,* 1, No. 3 (November, 1977–January, 1978), pp. 15–17.

Canter, Lee with Marlene Canter, *Assertive Discipline: A take-charge approach for today's educator.* Seal Beach, Cal.: Canter and Associates, Inc., 1976.

Cotler, Sherwin B. and Julio J. Guerra, *Assertion Training: A Humanistic-Behavioral Guide to Self Dignity.* Champaign, Ill.: Research Press, 1976.

"Dr. Frederic H. Jones—He's Got the Secret," *Creative Discipline: Searching for the better way,* 1, No. 6–7 (April–June, 1978), p. 16.

Lang, Arthur J. and Patricia Jakubowski, *Responsible Assertive Behavior: Cognitive/Behavioral Procedures for Trainers.* Champaign, Ill.: Research Press, 1976.

"Positive Peer Culture: a system based on Tender Loving Care," *Creative Discipline: Searching for the better way,* 1, No. 3 (November, 1977–January, 1978), pp. 5–6.

8 Positive Relationships with School Personnel and Parents

But understanding alone is not enough. When I understand something but do not put it into action, nothing has been accomplished either in the outside world or within myself.

Barry Stevens

Often the development of a positive personal relationship between parents and school personnel can be highly effective in dealing with inappropriate student behavior. As a teacher, you can use parents and other staff members as sounding boards, sources of information, and perhaps more objective evaluators of student behavior as well as your dealing with such behavior. Many times persons not immediately involved in a teacher–student power struggle can offer helpful suggestions that are not readily apparent to the participants.

Effectively enlisting the aid of others is primarily dependent upon the teacher answering three questions correctly:

1. Who should be involved in improving student behavior in this particular instance—the teacher alone, the parent, a particular staff member, or all three?

2. When should such assistance be sought?

3. How should the other persons be involved in trying to solve student education problems?

Too often a teacher mistakenly involves too many people or the wrong people in problem solving. Such mistakes can be avoided by carefully analyzing the situation at hand and correctly answering the above questions. The lines of communication that result from such analysis will be positive and extremely helpful in establishing a sound instructional/disciplinary program.

Who Should be Involved in Your Dealings with Student Behavior?

Putting your Trust in Fellow Teachers

It is a fact that most teachers, and more probably all teachers, will have difficulty handling a particular child or class at one time or another during their careers. Not allowing this difficulty to get to you and make you feel unsuccessful or anxious is an important step in becoming a self-sufficient, assured teacher. As stated previously, determining who can help you with problem student behavior when you no longer feel you are handling it correctly by yourself is a very important decision. The difficulty of making this decision is compounded if you are a recent addition to a teaching staff and unfamiliar with your fellow workers.

People generally seek advice from others who they feel are more proficient, experienced, or knowledgeable than themselves. Determining who is most proficient and knowledgeable among your acquaintances on the teaching staff can be tricky because you probably will have to rely upon hearsay. In few instances will you be allowed to actually see what occurs in the classroom next door once the door has been closed. You are more likely to witness other teachers dealing with group behavior outside of the classroom during assemblies, at recess, on bus duty or in the library. This may give you a false idea of their effectiveness in the classroom, because the techniques employed in crowd control may be inappropriate during classroom activities. (Relying on your Acme Thunderer Whistle indoors to get your students' attention can only mean that you are headed for trouble.)

Seeking help from the most experienced teacher (defining "experienced" as having taught for a number of years) is also not necessarily too effective. The fact that a person has taught for a long time does not mean that he or she is good at handling misbehavior. It may only mean that he or she has developed a thick skin and can put up with more or has learned to ignore misbehavior as it occurs. This is not effectively dealing with behavior. It's living with it.

Seeking help from experienced teachers is also becoming increasingly more difficult because the faculties are getting younger and have less experience, at least in terms of years of teaching. According to a recent National Education Association (NEA) survey of its members, the average teacher in 1976 was 33 years old, as compared to an average teacher in 1961 of 41 years of age with ten years of teaching experience. The younger faculties are not due to an increase of new teachers, but to the fact that more older teachers are leaving. The percentage of teachers with 20 or more years of experience is half of what it was fifteen years ago. It has dropped from 28% in 1961 to 14% in 1976. Younger teachers are frustrated and are saying that one cannot go to older teachers for help because they are also frustrated and ready to quit too. Such a situation obviously adversely affects the development of a referral source for inexperienced teachers.

Another problem encountered when determining which teachers can help you is that often the people most eager to advise are not the most qualified to do so. Very often the teacher who had great difficulty in handling student misbehavior during the first year of teaching, but managed to survive, will then go on in his second year to become the staff's master of discipline, shepherding the new teachers and offering advice at the drop of a hat. Hopefully, all involved will learn from the mistakes of the "rookie" and not repeat them. New teachers must also be wary of advisors who do not give completely honest advice and withhold important information. These pseudo-helpers may not intentionally try to make you fail, but they might like to see you learn through the difficult trial-and-error period that they suffered through themselves. The cliché "misery loves company" is often seen where individuals feel much better about their own failures if others fail also.

Although our previous remarks may not seem to favor approaching your fellow teachers for assistance, such is not the case. We only caution you not to seek assistance blindly. Before pouring out your problems to someone and expecting help from them, be fairly sure that they are reasonably capable and that they can be trusted to keep your problems confidential. The best help anyone can give you is to offer suggestions and refrain from spreading rumors of your ineffectiveness among the whole staff. Your success and stature on the staff may be dependent upon your avoidance of what we call the "foot-in-mouth" syndrome.

The foot-in-mouth syndrome can best be described as a teacher indiscreetly telling his or her problem in class control or complaining about an evaluating administrator to the wrong person. One common vehicle for this indiscretion is the teacher's lounge. If you are constantly complaining in the teacher's lounge about class disruptors or various problems, you may gain some vocal support but may eventually lose the respect of your fellow teachers. Gaining sympathy from others is not too positive if they draw the conclusion that you cannot do your job as well as they can. Broadcasting your predicament to a group of people in a crowded or noisy room may help start rumors about your ineffectiveness, based upon someone hearing only bits and pieces of conversations and misunderstanding what was said. If time runs out before you can completely discuss your problems or explain how you handled them, other teachers may mistakenly believe that you were unable to handle your students. Also, teacher's aides, volunteers, or other staff members overhearing only a part of the conversation may draw their own conclusions about your abilities and further add to the rumor mill in subsequent discussions. It is amazing how far and fast this kind of bad news can travel. Many a teacher's ability has been questioned and career jeopardized by carelessly talking to the wrong people at the wrong time.

Avoid attending your own teacher's lounge funeral by carefully choosing capable advisors who will really listen to your problems and offer helpful suggestions. This is best done in a fairly private place when you have enough time to clearly state the problem you are concerned about and to explore possible solutions. Participation in teacher lounge conversations is important if you want to be accepted by the staff and get to know the other teachers and ancillary personnel. Avoidance of the lounge is not recommended. However, if a problem area does arise during your dicussions with others, try not to dwell upon the negatives that you may be experiencing. Whenever possible, mention positive aspects of your teaching situation. Wait for the appropriate opportunity for discussing your problems. Most important, especially if you are new to the staff, listen carefully to the conversations of those around you. This will increase your chances for asking the correct person for help.

Developing a Positive Relationship with the Administrative Staff

The ability to choose the appropriate person to help you in dealing with disciplinary problems will be greatly determined by your knowledge of the school's administrative attitudes concerning student discipline. One of the first things you should do upon joining a school staff is to learn about the school's administration. If a school board policy book is available, study it to determine what the policies are concerning student behavior. If your school has a handbook, study it to learn school rules and established procedures for dealing with student behavior. Most important, become acquainted with your school's administrative staff. If the school is large, you may need to work with a number of persons in dealing with student misbehavior. In your conversations with the various administrators, try to determine whether they have a particular philosophy of, or methodology for, handling behavioral problems. Knowledge of their attitudes will give you insight into how they will feel about your behavioral management techniques and may help you to manage your class in a way that is most acceptable to them. You might also ask if they can recommend any teachers on the staff that you might talk to with reference to building upon your repertoire of good teaching ideas, as well as possible classroom management techniques. Besides finding a possible source of information, you will learn who the administrator considers to be a respected staff member doing a good job. There is nothing like modeling the behavior of the person who is considered to be the school loser for starting your career off on the wrong foot.

In talking with your principal, it is essential that you find out at what point he wants you to involve him or others if you experience classroom difficulties. Perhaps he feels that some other staff member, such as the school psychologist, assistant principal, counselor, or teacher should be consulted before he is involved. This is an extremely important question. Each school administrator has his or her own opinion of when a teacher should seek help. Some will want you to involve them in seemingly minor incidents. Others will want you to involve them only when bodily injury is imminent, and still others suggest that you involve them only when parents might get involved. The amount of administrative involvement is dependent upon the political scene of the school and the site administrator's own philosophy. Asking for help before it is too late is another example of anticipative action. Learning the site administrator's preferences is important, but you should not rigidly adhere to them if you are encountering serious difficulties in your classroom. If you have tried every technique you know and still have made no headway with the problem, you should feel comfortable in seeking assistance from your administration. You will be respected for having the intelligence to consult them before the problem is out of hand.

Once you have decided to ask for administrative assistance, you must try to communicate your needs without feeling as though you are admitting failure or presenting yourself as an insecure, or incompetent teacher. A forthright statement of the facts, including what has occurred, what you have done to stop the inappropriate behavior from recurring, and the students' reactions to these techniques will be much appreciated by the administrator. Your calmly and preparedly asking for professional assistance will be much more respected than covering up, constantly complaining or panicking. Hopefully, in response to your professionalism, the administrator will make suggestions or changes that would help you to improve your instructional program.

The development of a positive relationship with the administrative staff will be in part dependent upon your earliest dealings with them as well as your behavior during periods of stress. If you approach them positively and try to be a team member on the staff, you are more likely to receive their support when you need it. Such two-way support will help you both to be successful.

Parent-Teacher Communication and Student-Teacher Communication

Establishing rapport with parents is essential if a teacher wishes to call upon those parents to assist in the handling of their child's misbehavior. An effective relationship with parents has to be strong, positive and must avoid overrelying upon the old situations of "I'm going to tell your mommy" or "Wait until your father gets home." Parents know their children, and even if their love sometimes shadows their objectivity, they are more familiar with their child's school and medical history, and important influences at home than any person in the school scene. To learn valuable information that may give you insight into classroom problems or use parental pressure to help shape student behavior, you must get the parents to trust you. Unfortunately, you may find that, especially as the years pass and the number of school-home student conflicts increase, the parents may be suspicious of your motives, question your abilities, and, at times, support their children against you.

To help gain the support these parents can offer, and the insight into your students' behavior of which they may be aware, you must in turn be supportive of them. One good way of doing this is too keep them informed of their children's progress, or lack of it, in school. No one likes to be called upon to help solve a problem that has gotten out of hand. If you can reach a parent before a small problem has grown into a full-blown teacher-student power struggle, you will once again be practicing anticipative action. Contacting parents early will obviously not be possible with a one-time student blow up—a situation in which a student, for example, angrily calls you a name or hits someone for taunting him. However, contacting parents early when you feel that an inappropriate behavior pattern is becoming habitual, as in the case of students who are constantly fighting, abusive, destructive, or disruptive, is very important. Although less antisocial, other behaviors that are also unsettling for teachers are those that are related to school work, such as students who rarely come to school or class on time, finish assignments or come to class prepared with completed homework assignments and the necessary materials. (Many a teacher would probably give up a kingdom for some extra pencils when their students forget to bring them.) Hopefully, before calling about a problem, you will have already had some contact of a positive nature with the parents. Parents are more likely to work with you on a problem if they have met or spoken with you under more pleasant circumstances. Besides helping to establish rapport, such preliminary meetings will yield valuable information about parental attitudes and family history that may help you to determine whether the parents may be able and willing to help on future occasions.

If you have decided that parental help may be beneficial, then it is time for you to don the hat of a diplomat, not a prosecutor, and make your call. It is imperative that you calmly describe the situation, stressing the fact that you felt they are concerned parents and would want to be informed of any circumstances that may, if not changed, interfere with their child's progress or learning. The parents may be far more likely to work with you if you present the situation in this manner and then go on to say that you felt perhaps they could offer some information that might help to explain their child's change in behavior (if there has been a change) or the pattern of behavior you have observed. Besides helping you solve your school problems, your efforts together may also help the parents to handle similar behavior at home. Much negative behavior seen at school and at home may result from unfortunate or stressful circumstances in either place, and knowledge of such circumstances may greatly affect the way the student should be handled. In certain situations you may feel that additional help may be appropriate and wish to call in a resource person such as the school psychologist or counselor. Before doing this, however, you should check to see whether parental permission is mandatory. Thus, by carefully including the parents and instrumental ancillary personnel when necessary, you may be able to either stop the student's misbehavior or cope with an unchangeable behavior better in the future.

Positive Parent Conferencing

As we have stated earlier, good rapport with parents will, in part, be the result of your approaching them positively and keeping them informed of important events, good or bad, as they occur. Parents need, and generally want, to be informed of their child's progress. Today's parents, as a group, are better read and more sophisticated in terms of child rearing techniques than most of their predecessors and really want to know what is going on in the classroom. As parent education programs become more prevalent, parents are being better educated to deal with school problems. They are learning what questions they should ask to determine their child's progress. Also, parents are aware that their tax dollars support the school system and want educators to be held responsible for providing quality education. Such legislation as the Hart Act (1977) in California, requiring that all graduating students pass a proficiency examination in order to receive their high school diplomas, is evidence of this.

Parents and teachers working together can form the critical link that allows for the effective communication of student needs and problems. If either party is not properly informed and this lack of communication subsequently leads to disruptions of the educational development of the student, major educational goals may not be attained. Thus, the parent-teacher conference, whether successful or unsuccessful, will have important implications both for the student and teacher. Parents who are concerned and knowledgeable will generally attend a conference expecting information and the teacher should be prepared to inform them adequately. What questions will the parents ask? How should you answer and what purpose will your answers serve? These are important questions and will be answered in the following pages.

An example of the type and breadth of questions that parents could ask is illustrated in Table 8.1 by the list of questions developed by a school psychologist, Robert Joy.

Table 8.1   Parent Concerns

Questions that are likely to be asked during parent-teacher conferences

1. What is your policy of homework?
2. What is your grading policy?
3. How are my child's fine motor skills?
4. How are my child's gross motor skills?
5. How was my child's adjustment to your program or class?
6. Does my child start, continue, and complete assignments?
7. Is my child organized?
8. Will my child ask for help when necessary?
9. Does my child work well in a group activity?
10. Is my child responsible?
11. Is my child able to do things independently?
12. Does my child play with children his/her own age?
13. How does my child handle being disciplined?
14. How are my child's secretarial skills?
15. What is my child's skill level in reading? Spelling? Math?
16. What can my child do now that he/she could not do before coming into your class or program?
17. Will my child be successful next year?
18. What can I do to support my child's school experience?

The purpose of this conference sheet is to give structure and guidelines to the conference itself. The valuable time you spend with parents should enhance your communication with them, not confuse them. If you do not know what to say or what questions to ask, the conference time will usually be spent unproductively. You should not discuss your personal problems, the parent's personal problems or any problem that is unrelated to the particular child under discussion. You should especially avoid discussing any past experiences you may have had with this child's brothers or sisters whom you may have had previously in class.

Being prepared to answer these questions or to present this information without being asked will help make your parent-teacher conferences positive and student-oriented. It will also help to satisfy both parental and teacher needs for information. The time you spend with parents is designed to acquaint them with your basic educational beliefs as well as to develop an alliance which is aimed at your better educating their child. The knowledge you present when you are prepared to answer these questions is very important. It tells the parents that you do, indeed, know their child and will make them more confident in your ability to teach their child effectively. We will discuss each of the parental concern questions to emphasize specific teaching rationale and the aspects of the questions that are most beneficial for you and the parents to discuss in your attempt to avoid and solve problems.

1. What is your homework policy?

Although you may regard homework as a minor part of your educational program and place little emphasis on it, most parents are very concerned about homework. Since homework is the only actual school work that they will see done, they will tend to judge what is going on in the classroom from what they see or do not see at home. Thus, you must clearly communicate what your policy is towards homework. Hopefully, your discussion with the parents will prevent the student from turning a simple ten- or fifteen-minute homework assignment into two hours of family disruption.

In general, homework should be used to reinforce learning that has occurred during the day. Although older and more advanced students may be able to work independently on new projects at home, generally new subject matter should not be sent home with your students to learn after school. Both students and parents could be frustrated by difficult or unfamiliar homework assignments. Sharing with parents your expectations for completion of homework assignments may help you to avoid additional conflicts. Also stating your rationale for using specific techniques when appropriate may stop the parents from introducing confusing techniques or subject matter to their children.

Parent conferences can correct many misunderstandings about homework practices. Alerting parents, as well as students, to the importance of long term assignments, in advance whenever possible, can lower the number of heated or anxious phone calls you will receive from parents whose children have left work to the last minute. Mentioning major assignments at back to school night or giving parents a calendar of activities and important assignments may help reduce the number of students bringing home stacks of books on Thursday night and saying they will fail if they do not read them all by the next day. If you expect work to be done at home, it is not unreasonable to let the parents know of your expectations. Such information will prevent many misunderstandings and assist parents who are interested to help their children be more successful.

In general, homework assignments should not be too lengthy, perhaps no longer than 15 minutes for primary grades and 20 to 30 minutes in the upper elementary grades. If you teach in a departmentalized setting or in a junior high school where students move from class to class, you must also be careful of the length of homework assignments. If four teachers make one-hour-long assignments each on the same night, the student will be faced with an overwhelming amount to do. If a parent complains, feeling too much time is being spent by the student doing homework, it is clearly time for the two of you to investigate the cause of this.

2. What is your grading policy?

The responsibility of communicating grading policy is clearly one that must be undertaken early in the school year. So much confusion is generated between parent and teacher as to what grades really mean. Parents are usually not aware that there is in essence no standardized policy of grading. This is especially true in programs for the handicapped.

Report cards are a direct reflection of grading policy. Often parents will assume that their children's grades mean the same as theirs did when they were children. This is not necessarily true. The recent trend in grading is to narratively describe the students' behavior and skills achieved. You must communicate to the parents your interpretation of the purpose and meaning of the grades you give your students. Since grading is a purely subjective statement of the child's accomplishment of what the teacher feels is important, it is crucial that you explain to parents, as well as to students, what you stress in your program. If you do not communicate this, the parent may think you use the same grading policies as did last year's teacher. Making parents aware of your attitudes and practices prior to the child bringing home a poor report card may alleviate much confusion and angry phone calls.

3. How are my child's fine motor skills?

The teacher is best qualified to determine the students' level of development of fine motor skills. Establishing expectation levels for your students' growth in this area is only feasible when you have evaluated their work. Due to the developmental aspects of fine motor skills, your evaluations and expectations should be geared toward quality, not quantity, of effort.

Children who are delayed in fine motor skill development are often easily discouraged about completing assignments. They need understanding and support and must also be exposed to activities which will improve and further develop fine motor coordination.

Since children with fine motor delays are often wrongly expected by teachers and parents to perform as well as any other child of their age group, discussion of this problem in parent-teacher conferences may help relieve unfair demands upon the student and tensions of the parents or teacher. You may encounter many students whose behavioral outbursts are due to their frustrations over inadequate skills. You should remember that when you ask a student to copy the math problems from a book, for example, you might be giving the student a fine motor skill assignment that he or she might not be able to perform despite his or her mathematical competency. If they refuse to do the work, fool around, or angrily act out, you must deal with the appropriate cause of these problems. Such complicated behavior should be brought to the parents' attention so that all concerned will understand the impact of appropriately dealing with such behavior.

4. How are my child's gross motor skills?

Gross motor skills are usually evidenced during play or physical education activities. You should communicate to the parents the student's levels of development that you have observed and the plan that you have for enhancing those skills, if appropriate.

Gross motor skill development often correlates with a child's social development. A student who possesses good gross motor skills is often accepted by his peers as being "one of the gang." When gross motor skills are delayed, then the self-esteem of the student is often low because of not fitting in with the rest of the class.

Another ramification of a student's gross motor skill development is that if the skills are delayed, the student is not likely to be motivated to do those activities that will enhance the development of the gross motor muscles. You need to have a plan that will keep the student involved in the program moving towards adequate strength, conditioning and development.

Discussion of a child's gross motor skills may become even more important as a child grows older. Many parents may complain that their child is just plain clumsy and they get so tired of his or her falling over objects or knocking things over. Some behavior problems can be prevented by teachers training children to walk down the hall without bumping into other students. Since motor development is so important, both teachers and parents should be interested in helping children to improve in both fine and gross motor capacities. The observations of teachers and parents will also be instrumental in spotting motoric deficiencies that may need to be corrected by medical personnel.

5. How was my child's adjustment to your program or class?

Adjustments to a new class or program is the parents' barometer as to the social development of the student. Students who have adjustment problems upon entering new situations need special attention and concern.

Parents and teachers should develop close communication so that the student's encounter with a new situation is accepting and warm. Preventive approaches to children with special emotional needs necessitate that all people who will come in contact with them both at home and at school know what sets them off, or even more important, what works. Only through communication with appropriate people can corrective measures be implemented.

A discussion of the child's adjustment to school will help the parent learn how his child adjusts to new situations and groups of people. This discussion may hold surprises for both teacher and parents. One child may be a complete extrovert at home and an introvert at school, while another child might be a quiet bookworm at home and the class clown at school. Determining which, if either, behavior type is more desirable and the circumstances in which the opposing behaviors occur will be valuable in terms of learning teacher and parent preferences as well as possible avenues of modifying less desirable or inappropriate behaviors in the classroom. Such discussion will also prevent teacher and parents from getting a false picture of what is happening at home and at school. Since a child's success both in school and out is greatly determined by his ability to react well to new or different situations, this is a crucial area to explore with parents.

6.   Does my child start, continue, and complete assignments?

The student's assignment, or task, completion is another important topic to discuss with parents. Special attention must be given to those students who have difficulty starting a task. It requires a positive approach by all concerned to get the student to begin to work. It is not enough to be content with the student initiating a task. The student, if he is to be successful in school, must continue towards the completion of the task. If these conditions occur on a relatively inconsistent basis, the teacher must reinforce the child when appropriate behavior is exhibited. Completion of tasks gives the student a sense of self-worth and accomplishment.

Many times children will start an activity and then stop, start again, and stop. They start and stop so often that they are unable to complete the assignment. Other students start and stop and then rush to finish the assignment at the very last minute, usually resulting in messy, error-ridden work. The general quality of the work, as well as the amount of production, can be improved if the teacher works on the student's task completion. In discussing the importance of task completion with parents, the teacher may find out that the child has trouble with task completion at home. Perhaps by working together, the parent and teacher can help the student to better attend to tasks. Often the reason students do not complete assignments is that they lack knowledge of how to proceed in an organized manner. Parents and teachers are generally concerned with the subject matter that is being taught but the teacher must be equally concerned with how the student learns, if learning problems are to be lessened. Teaching students to work toward target objectives is an important job of the teacher and your efforts in this area should be explained to the parents.

7. Is my child organized?

An essential element of student success in school is their level of organization. This will be demonstrated by how they approach tasks as well as how they complete them. Accomplishing tasks in an organized manner is done by breaking down the task into components and accomplishing each component in sequence moving from the least to the most complex or sophisticated. The more organized a student is, the more productive he will be in school. Being a productive student would include such things as coming into a classroom, exhibiting appropriate student behavior, sitting down, putting things away, sharing, participating appropriately, and by delaying gratification.

A student's organization or lack of it should not come as a surprise to parents. A quick look inside the student's desk or locker or bedroom at home will tell a great deal about his proficiency in this area. If they both look like the site of a major World War II battle, you know that this student needs help in this area. If one is good, while the other is bad, however, you and the parents should try to determine what causes this disparity.

8. Will my child ask for help when necessary?

Asking for help appropriately is also an essential skill that must be mastered if a student is to profit from the educational experience to the greatest extent possible. Some students have mastered this skill to a high degree, others are so discouraged that they somehow appear to be immobilized in regards to asking for help. You as the teacher must also be aware that a student can abuse this skill by seeking attention through the media of asking for help. Appropriate requests for help is the issue.

Establishing an environment that is supportive of student requests for help is the key. A teacher must be close by in order to respond quickly, therefore, reinforcing the student to ask for help. Fearing failure, criticism, or even attention from a stranger (the teacher), introverted children may either vegetate or attempt to do a task that they do not know how to do. Once you have discovered such a child, a conference with the parents may be extremely helpful to uncover the reasons for such fear. Obviously a child who is so shy will probably not be able to discuss the problem with you adequately. The parent may also be able to suggest ways that will help bring the child out as well as provide support and reinforcement from the home. In such cases, a home-school contract or even a note from the teacher commending the student's asking for help when needed may be good motivators.

9. Does my child work well in a group activity?

A child working well in group activities may be related to his or her over-all adjustment to school. Discussions along these lines, besides pointing out the degree of success a child has in groups, will also show the parent the variety of activities that you have planned and the importance of group work in your classroom. Gauging the students' security in both individual and group situations is an important teacher task if he or she is to teach to all the students' needs.

The definition of a group is two or more individuals. The ability to work well in a group activity is again essential to the career of any student. Therefore, if the student does not have the ability to work with two other students, for example, then he or she should not be expected to work with a group of ten. The teacher needs to set up the learning environment that will lend itself to the development of students working in larger and larger groups. Careful selection by the teacher in forming a group of students is the key to the development of this skill.

10. Is my child responsible?

A child's sense of responsibility should not be too much of a surprise to parents because they constantly give their children assignments at home which demonstrate their responsibility. Noting that conferences are for telling the good as well as the bad, teachers may be able to comment on an increase in the child's responsible behavior in class from the beginning of the year to the end. Deciding what constitutes responsible behavior may be a very subjective matter. Before a discussion on this subject is begun, care should be taken to state what both parents and teachers mean by responsible so that misunderstandings can be avoided.

Activities that promote responsible behavior, such as the student turning in a completed assignment, or remembering to bring required materials to class, give the teacher the opportunity to reinforce the student either through encouragement or praise. Responsibility can be learned if the teacher sets up the environment so that the student will be exposed to greater and greater degrees of responsibility.

11. Is my child able to do things independently?

The answer to this question will be closely related to the answers of the last six questions. Independent function will result when the student can initiate and complete activities appropriately, when he or she is not afraid to ask for help, can work well with others, and is responsible. Since a student will not learn to function independently unless he or she is given the opportunity to work or play without constant supervision, both parent and teacher may, through their discussion, be able to discover new ways of giving the student necessary freedom both at school and at home.

12. Does my child play with children his/her own age?

A teacher needs to be aware of the student's friends or playmates. Observing the student in unstructured play activities, such as recess, give clues as to the student's social development. Generally, children play with other children their own age or approximately their own age. A teacher should promote this similar age play activity.

A teacher who consistently observes a student playing with other children three and four years older or younger should be aware that when there is an age span of two or three years, the relationship between the children is often exploitive. The older child will often manipulate the younger child into doing things that are not in the second child's best interests. An older child who seeks out younger children as playmates will often do this because he or she cannot find children his own age to play with, either because there are not any in the group or because he or she has been rejected by the group. This is often accompanied by a poor self-image and feelings of inadequacy.

The teacher must establish a plan that will allow the student to function with similar aged peers. This may mean assigning a child to play with other children nearer the child's age. It may mean preventing the older child from playing or seeking out younger children. The teacher can do this by structuring recess or lunch period with planned activities.

13. How does my child handle being disciplined?

Children do not learn alike and will not respond to disciplinary measures in the same way. Some children may cry when scolded, others may be overtly defiant, and still others may meekly accept whatever is said or done to them. The most appropriate response to discipline is improved behavior or cessation of the misbehavior. Many parents may be eager to find out what you do to make their children behave if they are encountering behavioral problems at home. On the other hand, you must be prepared to defend your actions if parents take exception to your methodology. Parental reaction to disciplinary measures can be as individual as their childrens'—making this part of the conference unpredictable.

There are two major reasons for including this question in the list of parental concerns. The first is for the teacher to learn from the parent just what form of discipline, if any, works with the student at home. Secondly, observing this reaction allows the teacher to ascertain the social development of the student. A student who displays angry, disruptive behavior over a minor disciplinary incident may be in need of much help. In contrast, the child who accepts the disciplinary action as being appropriate, is well on the way towards responsible student behavior.

14. How are my child's secretarial skills?

Secretarial skills are defined as the ability of the student to complete paperwork assigned. Unfortunately, much that is asked of a student is in fact secretarial work (busywork) and is not truly reflective of learning. Students who are able to complete great amounts of paperwork are often viewed by the teacher as being good learners. Learning is defined as a change of behavior. Completion of paperwork does not necessarily mean the student has learned or profited from the experience. Teachers, as well as parents, must keep this in mind when it comes to making an appropriate evaluation of the student's progress (grading).

15. What is my child's skill level in reading? Spelling? Math?

So much emphasis is presently being placed on group and individual achievement tests that it should not be a difficult task to present to the parent the skill level the student possesses in the above categories, as well as in additional categories. A teacher should also indicate to the parent what is meant by grade level scores and also by percentiles.

The parent of a child should never be surprised as to the exact level of functioning by the child. When a parent is presented with skill level scores, then all the parent has to do is compare the present scores with previous scores to determine if the student is making progress.

16. What can my child do now that he/she could not do before coming into your class or program?

In order to respond to this question, a teacher must have completed some type of pretesting and recorded the results. It is not absolutely necessary for post testing to have been completed but generally it is a good idea. A valid response to this question usually comes only after the teacher has worked with a child for a long period of time. Three-quarters of a school year is a minimum time expectancy. This question lies at the very heart of the purpose for education. Good record keeping and monitoring of the student's progress automatically allows the teacher to have this type of information available for the parent upon request. For example:

Reading Recognition:
> 4.1 Wide Range Achievement Test
> Administered on 9-18-76

Reading Recognition:
> 5.7 Wide Range Achievement Test
> Administered on 5-18-77
> ___
> 1.6 Grade levels growth in nine months of instruction.

17. Will my child be successful next year?

As we all know, teachers cannot generally read crystal balls. So this question will be a difficult one to answer. However, many times parents need the reassurance that their child is making adequate progress to be promoted. You, as the teacher, need to make this professional judgment and be able to share this judgment with the parent. There is no guarantee that a child will be successful the following year, and if there is doubt the parent should be informed. It is unfair to both student and parents to pass a student along year after year and then, when the child is about to graduate, the parents are told that their child is reading at a second grade level, spelling at a second grade level, and computing arithmetic at a third grade level. This is a difficult and demoralizing surprise for everyone concerned.

18. What can I do to support my child's school experience?

Explaining how parents may be able to support their children in school will be very much dependent upon the student's individual needs. However, encouraging parents to maintain lines of communication with you will be very supportive for them, you, and for the students. Teachers should not avoid dealing with parents. On the contrary, even parental criticism of the educational program shows concern over the quality of their child's education and the parents should be commended for their interest. Keeping the parents informed of classroom events, student progress and your objectives can help them to stay up-to-date with the important concerns of their children and reinforce their children's efforts. Your willingness to include the parents in enjoyable activities as well as problem solving sessions will make them want to become more involved in your class and possibly in the entire school.

Teachers should cautiously approach asking parents to assist in teaching their child needed skills. Due to their subjective relations and evaluations of their own children, they may encounter great difficulties in instructing their own children (even when they are quite capable of teaching someone else's children).

Open communication between the parents and the teacher is the real key in parent-teacher conferences. Including parents in decision making experiences helps give them a real sense of meaning and participation. Encouraging the parents to notify you when something is going well at home is just as important as being informed when something is not going satisfactorily.

The answers to these questions can give both teachers and parents real insight into the educational, emotional, and social development of the student. How many times a year the parents need to sit down with the teacher to discuss these matters depends on the student's needs. Perhaps one question could be asked weekly until it was no longer necessary to ask that question. This is just one aspect of individualization of the teaching and communication process that must occur in a successful classroom.

In summary then, we must state that positive interpersonal relationships are best developed by establishing a program of two-way support based on effective communication practices. Barriers to providing an excellent educational program are not due as much to teaching inabilities as they are to communication dysfunctions. Striving to inform all interested parties in a professional, clearminded manner will reap many benefits in terms of needed information and support. With administrative, staff, and parental support, the teacher then will be more able to develop a strong instructional program and handle disciplinary problems much more effectively.

1.   Presented with the following description of an incident in your class, how would you proceed? Do you feel you need help? Who would you ask for help—parents, teachers, counselors, or the principal? When would be the best time to contact them?

You have taken roll, started your students on their written assignment when John, age 13, saunters in eight minutes late, totally unprepared to work. This is the third time this week that John has come to class without pencil or books. You ask John to explain why he's late and where his materials are, and he tells you that it's none of your business. You tell him that such insolence is uncalled for and he profanely tells you to shut up.

2.   In the previous incident, the principal calls you in two days later to say that John's parents feel that you are being unfair to him and embarrassed him in front of the class. He wants you to explain why parents are complaining to him before you spoke to him about it? What will you say?

3.   You have been having difficulties with one of the students in your class and have set up a parent-teacher conference for the next day. That night the student calls you at home, tells you that she'll never do the wrong things again and begs you not to tell her parents of her behavior or of her calling you. What do you do?

Bibliography

Buscaglia, Leo, *The Disabled and Their Parents: a counseling challenge*. Thorofare, N.J.: Charles B. Slack, Inc., 1975, p. 39.

9 Attaining and Retaining Teaching Positions

You never get a second chance to make a first good impression.

Source Unknown

The reader might well ask, "Why include information about attaining and retaining teaching positions in a book relating to classroom discipline?" The reasons are important, because underlying major classroom discipline problems are the inner and, many times, unspoken tensions of the teacher. These anxieties and tensions stem in part from the pressures which are placed on teachers because of intensified efforts to evaluate teachers in more measurable terms. School districts and teacher organizations throughout the country have been called upon to create perfect rating systems and evaluation forms. Teacher organizations in New York, Ohio, Michigan, and California, as well as in many other states, are becoming increasingly involved in a titanic struggle regarding the scope of collective bargaining. Teachers who have been dismissed because of poor evaluations consistently feel they have been wronged and management was incorrect. Whether you are a new teacher, a veteran, or a person looking for a firsttime position, you will, during your career, feel these pressures and they are bound to have an effect, direct or indirect, upon your school and classroom environment. If you can develop some inner peace of mind and stability as a professional in these areas, you will be free to expend more of your energy and effort in the teaching-learning process. This chapter will address itself to techniques which will enable the teacher to cope with the twin pressures of teacher evaluation and collective bargaining.

Coping with Teacher Evaluations

First, let us deal with teacher evaluation pressures and how to ease them. Notice we said ease them, not eliminate them, since it is obvious that taxpayers, parents, school boards, and state legislatures will continue to exert pressures to perfect the system. At the onset, it is self-evident that the teacher, through the teacher organization, should play an essential part in the construction or revision of any teacher evaluation system. Current California law (1978) for example, *requires* that this procedure be followed.

Assuming that teachers are, or have been, involved in this process, should they then sequester themselves in their classrooms, happy and euphoric in the feeling they have at last relieved their major source of anxiety? No teacher with any degree of intelligence can subscribe to this point of view. It is apparent that, even though current evaluation systems are not perfect, they do represent existing policy and procedure. Rather than continually find fault and be outraged, it is infinitely more desirable for one's peace of mind to work within the system.

This means that you as a teacher should scrupulously abide by existing deadlines each step of the way. In fact, if you are particularly prone to psychological stress, it is highly advisable to meet all deadlines *well in advance.* If your supervisor is not complying with policy, a gentle reminder (in writing) should be given by you. This is essential (always keep a copy in your files) since legal procedures require evidence in writing of any discrepancy in the existing policy. It will also help you to feel more secure, knowing that you have no reason to feel guilty because of lack of compliance on your part. Since evaluation is a fact of life why not be prepared for other possible options. Such preparation can be a great comfort in time of need and other times as well.

Let us now turn to one area of preparation which virtually 90% of the profession chooses to ignore. Reference here is made to the fact that teachers rarely keep their professional papers and resumés up to date. A worse problem arises when on certain rare occasions, papers are submitted as part of a job application which are unorganized, have grammatical and spelling errors, lack specific detail that relates to the job that is desired, and almost always are out of date. In the fall of 1976, a major western university placement center wrote to some 700 employers, many of whom had been coming twice a year to the campus, to recruit graduates for business, industry, education, and government. They were asked whether they were satisfied with the writing skills of the graduates who were now in their employ. Their responses were rather startling:

Twenty-one percent (21%) of the 150 who replied rated graduates as poor letter writers. Twenty percent (20%) considered them unable to prepare reports properly, mostly because of lack of organization. Thirty percent (30%) categorized graduates as *poor spellers.* One out of five respondents also stated that the graduates were "incapable of good rhetoric," i.e., inarticulate.

The message is clear. Prepare your papers scrupulously, attend to each detail and be sure you proof-read them before they are sent to a potential employer.

Papers should contain at least three current references from *immediate* supervisors who have *direct* knowledge of your ability. This requires you to ask the principal, a fellow teacher, and perhaps a district curriculum supervisor or superintendent to write a reference related to your performance on the job.

"Won't this jeopardize my current employment?" you might ask. We have talked to several personnel directors who steadfastly maintain that you have an obligation to yourself to request these references on a year-to-year basis. How many of us have delayed asking for a reference until it is too late—perhaps that principal who thought so much of you has been transferred or has taken another job out of state or maybe has passed on to "that little red schoolhouse in the sky." Be assured that keeping your professional papers updated is one positive thing which you can do to help lessen your anxiety in time of stress. If you've never pulled together a set of papers, you may now be asking, "What procedure should you follow as you apply for your first job or your next promotional opportunity?" The following section will answer this question.

What To Do When Applying for Your First or Next Job

Step 1: Prepare a Resumé

A well-prepared resumé can be mailed to many school districts without the time and cost required to visit each one personally. Do not overlook the chance to personally deliver your resumé if the situation warrants it. Your resumé must represent you accurately and adequately.

Typewritten resumés are preferred, but Xerox copies are useful and less costly if multiple copies are necessary. The resumé should be limited to two pages (certainly never more than three pages). It is also imperative to include a short letter of application to send with your resumé. (See appendix at the end of this chapter.) In your letter you should request a formal application blank which you should complete and return as soon as possible. Most personnel officers do not acknowledge receipt of resumés unless applicants are inquiring about specifically advertised positions.

Proofread the materials, making sure that every word is spelled correctly, that there are no typing errors, that margins are correct, and that the resumé is generally pleasing to the eye and catches the attention of the reader. Who might this reader be? It could be a clerk typist, an executive secretary, a personnel director or assistant, a committee of teachers, a principal, or a superintendent, or any combination of the above.

The following material should be included in any basic resumé (see appendix at the end of chapter for sample):

Personal Data. Name, home and business address, business and home phone, date of birth, citizenship, ethnicity, marital status.

Date of birth, citizenship, ethnicity, marital status are all optional, but should be included if they are advantageous to the applicant. For example, if the district is highly conservative and you are happily married with two children, be sure to include that data. If you recently divorced, do not include marital status. If the district is looking for bilingual applicants and your ethnicity is Mexican-American and you speak Spanish, the inclusion of this kind of data is vital. If, on the other hand, you come from an Anglo background, speak only English, do not include citizenship and ethnicity.

What about including a picture? Once again, if it is to your advantage, include a color photo, taken by a professional photographer. If you are in doubt, do not include the picture. Remember your sole purpose is to get an interview. Your papers are your passport to get through the myriads of screening devices, committees, and diverse personnel whose major function is to recommend a dozen or so "qualified" applicants for interviews with an ultimate decision-maker. Do not forget that your papers must compete with scores (sometimes hundreds) of equally qualified applicants and therefore must literally have neon lights on in order to stand up against the competition. The only control you exert is what you do in advance.

Professional Experience. List all experiences, particularly as they relate to the position. Be specific about the dates and places worked. Include a brief description of the job and start with the most recent position and proceed in reverse order to the first position held:

As an example:

> 1976 to present—Social studies teacher, grades 9, 10
> Oak Glen Unified School District
> Oak Glen, Oklahoma

> 1974–1976   —English teacher, grade 8
> Stevenville Elementary School District
> Stevenville, California

So you are applying for your first job—what professional experience have you had? Plenty. Be sure to list your student teaching experience in considerable detail. What about special research projects or papers which you have prepared while working on your degree? If these are appropriate, include them. Special workshops attended or participation in outstanding seminars may also be appropriate. It is essential to "flesh out" this section if your application is to be given any consideration. Three to five items are sufficient. More than five are superfluous.

Education. Once again, list your degrees starting with the most recent. List the university or college, the degree, date conferred, and major field of study. Also be sure to list graduate courses beyond the degree and dates of completion.

As an example:

> 1975—Northwestern University, M.A.
> Major: Special Education

> 1970—University of Illinois, A.B.
> Major: English

Credentials. List credentials received with date of expiration or whether they are issued for life. Also state what the credential authorizes you to teach.

For example:

General Elementary:	Expiration date 1983;
(Ohio)	Authorizes service as a teacher in grades K-8
Special Education:	Life; Authorizes service as a teacher for
(California)	educationally handicapped, educable mentally
	retarded, and trainable mentally retarded.

The authorization is usually printed on the face of the document. If you are not sure, ask for an interpretation from your personnel department or state credentialing agency.

Selected Accomplishments and Honors. This section is designed to allow you to "toot your own horn" but not too obviously. Do not exaggerate but state factually honors you have been awarded. Accomplishments outside the field of education should be included here.

Sometimes applicants label this section "Other Experiences" or "Selected Achievements." Use your own creative sense, keep it factual, but do not include every minor award you have received in your lifetime since grade six, such as head cheerleader in high school, lineman of the week, best apple bobber, etc.

For example:

- Graduated with distinction from Pennsylvania State University, June, 1970.

- Two year university scholarship awarded by the Pennsylvania Association for Retarded Children 9/68–6/70.

- Graduated with 3.73 G.P.A. from Pennsylvania State University, 1970

- Station Manager, Radio Station WGHB-FM Pennsylvania State University.

References. Include the names of three to five people who know of your work. Include name, title, place of employment, address, and business and home phone numbers.

The inclusion of phone numbers is especially important. Someone reading your file is not going to bother looking up phone numbers. Yet, this important item is left off because the applicant generally does not want to take time to look it up and include it. Be sure to talk to all the people you intend to use as a reference in advance, asking if you may use their name. Generally personnel directors will call one or two references who know directly of your work. They are not too interested in your local minister, your professor (with certain exceptions) or your local doctor.

In the education business, it is necessary to maintain this file at a local university or college. Local means somewhere within the state where you can have access by phone or by personal visit. Frequently, time constraints will not allow an applicant to get this vital data in the hands of the appropriate decisionmaker if the materials are safely filed in a university placement center some two to three thousand miles away. Universities maintain reciprocal arrangements which allow you to have your papers available at a local educational placement agency.

It should also be noted that placement bureaus require additional details, such as coursework completed, units achieved, grade point averages. This needs to be taken care of well in advance of any serious job application. It is also important for the applicant to have several (three to five) reference letters on file. These may or may not be confidential and should correspond to the references listed in your resumé. This entire package is what is known as your set of confidential papers. It is the *responsibility of the applicant* to make sure these papers are on the desk of the personnel director well in advance of the deadline established for those who are applying for the position. A knowledgeable applicant will call (preferably in person) the personnel director to make sure the papers are received and everything is in order. It also may be necessary to check with your placement bureaus to determine the quality of your placement papers. Can they be easily read, or are the copies "fuzzy" or unclear?

The intelligent applicant leaves no stone unturned in his or her quest to make the application stand out. For example, the use of buff or "off white" paper sometimes helps. Why not put each paper in a thin clear plastic folder and include all of the papers in a neat folder? Remember, the sole purpose here is to get to the interviews. To do this your papers must be outstanding. Occasionally personal calls to the right decisionmaker can be helpful although this technique can sometimes backfire. The applicant will have to use careful discretion and judgment in these matters, but it is wise to at least consider this option.

Step 2: The Interview

Once you successfully pass the paper screening, you are ready for the interview, or more correctly, a series of interviews. The first interview, time permitting, will generally be conducted by the personnel director or his/her assistant. During this first interview, you will probably be asked some general questions based on your resumé such as:

"What special contributions can you make to this school district?"

"What grade level do you feel most competent to teach? Why?"

"Tell me about your student teaching experience."

As these questions are asked, judgments will be made about your personality, your appearance, interpersonal relationships, etc.

Speaking of appearance, while it seems obvious, it should be stated that the way you dress is extremely important. Casual clothes, pant suits, sport shirts, unkempt hair, untrimmed beards, etc. are definitely out of place. Dresses for women, and suits and ties for men are a must if you want to convey a professional attitude and be considered for the next interview with the principal and/or local school committee. During this stage, fellow teachers will have a chance to test your knowledge and understanding of what happens in the classroom. You may be asked to teach a short lesson with "real live kids" or you may be videotaped. You will certainly be asked more specific questions such as:

"Do you prefer the open or more traditional classroom environment?"

"How would you use a teacher aide most effectively?"

"You have a student who is excellent academically, but consistently tardy. What would you do?"

"How do you handle serious discipline problems? Give me an example."

"How do you motivate students to learn?"

"Do you believe in team teaching?"

For additional sample questions, see *Thinking it Through* at the end of this chapter.

If you have done your homework, you will know what type of philosophy of education prevails in a given school or district and thus be better able to field the questions which are asked. If you have made a good impression on the teacher committee, the principal may want to talk to you privately. Once again, the principal's questions will reflect a particular philosophy which you should be able to detect. He or she will be considerably influenced by the opinions of his staff, so you would be well advised to give some *sincere* compliments about the school, staff, students, etc. At no time should you be untruthful or insincere in your answers, but it is important to the principal that a potential staff member be able to be compatible and to work with parents, teachers, and staff. He or she also wants to be assured that you have excellent classroom management. He or she generally wants a person with good common sense and strong up-to-date knowledge of what is happening in the field of education. If you have a particular strength, perhaps recent training in dealing with remedial reading problems, you should be sure to call this to the attention of your interviewers. Be sure to work it in without being too obvious. No one likes a braggart, but conversely, "shrinking violets" are also not held in great esteem.

Some additional notes about interviews are in order. Most people are quite nervous at the prospect of an interview—and this is natural—after all, the stakes are high. How then can one handle this situation? The best way is to carefully prepare in advance.

For a start, be sure you know your resumé. Do some role playing with a friend. Have your friend do the interviewing. Practice with three or four teacher-friends who can simulate a committee interview. Once your real interview begins, you will tend to relax and enjoy it. If you have prepared well, you will receive great satisfaction and indeed, even be surprised about your professional storehouse of knowledge and the quality of your answers, even when the questions are complex and difficult. If the question seems impossible or obtuse, ask your interviewer to rephrase, or better still, repeat the question in your own words asking, "Is that what you mean?" This will also give you some precious time to collect your thoughts and give a more coherent answer.

It is not a good practice to jump in with an immediate answer or to anticipate what the questioner has in mind before he or she completes the entire question. In other words, don't interrupt. Occasionally, after you have answered the question, you might say, "Have I answered your question, Mr. _____?" Interviewers appreciate courtesy and such a question gives them a chance to rephrase if necessary.

The following list of dos and don'ts for interviewees is designed to be used as a guideline for maximizing your success during your interviews.

The Interview: A List of Dos and Don'ts

Do

1. Come to the interview fully prepared.

2. Be on time, even ten minutes early. If detained, call ahead and try to set up another appointment.

3. Go to the interview with confidence.

4. Bring extra copies of your resumé. Make them available for any additional members of the interviewing panel.

5. Think before you speak and respond to all questions clearly and succinctly.

6. Be yourself, relaxed and self-confident.

7. Be specific, not vague, in your responses or statements.

8. Look directly at your interviewers as you speak or respond.

9. Use discretion when speaking about former employers, supervisors, or fellow teachers.

10. Thank the interviewers after the session.

Don't

1. Load down your resumé with unnecessary details or statements.

2. Leave gaps in the resumé.

3. Talk too much during the interview.

4. Repeat yourself.

5. Ask about working hours, holidays, sick leave and similar fringe benefits. This is better done before or after the interview.

6. Prolong the interview or attempt to get a positive commitment from the interviewer.

7. Smoke, chew gum, or fiddle with objects in your hand.

8. Wear dark sunglasses.

9. Dress in far-out fashions for the interview.

10. Go to the interview accompanied by friends or relatives.

In summary, please remember that interviewers want you to do your best. Perhaps your answers indicate a philosophical difference which in no way negates your ability as a strong teacher. It is in the interest of both parties to discover such important differences prior to making any permanent employment decisions. In such a situation, you are actually better off when you are not chosen for a position that has the potential for placing you in an awkward or unsupported position in the future. The fact that you know your papers are up-to-date and you have an option to apply for other positions if necessary will certainly have a positive day-to-day effect on your teaching-learning environment.

The Teacher's Recourse When Problems Arise

Next we would like to discuss the effects of membership in teacher organizations, when or whether to file a grievance, and teacher rights. In our discussion we are again aiming at your achieving peace of mind throughout your daily teaching activities. One of the first important noninstructional decisions you will make after being hired as a teacher is whether to join or not join your local teacher organization. This is, of course, a very personal matter, and in these times, may constitute a serious financial consideration for you. As a member of the profession, it may seem both logical and beneficial to involve yourself in the activities of the profession. While you may not agree with everything that is done by the teacher organization, you certainly are in no position to influence decisions from outside the local organization.

If you do decide to join, remembering you are not obligated to do so unless it is so stated in the agreement, you have an important voice in determining what your leadership should be doing in recommending inclusion of such things as class size, evaluation procedures, and fringe benefits in the annual negotiated agreement. States such as Illinois, Ohio, Pennsylvania, Michigan, Massachusetts, Connecticut, New York, New Jersey, and California have through their state legislatures approved the establishment of collective bargaining agreements between local districts and teacher organizations. In fact, the majority of school districts in the country today operate under some kind of collective bargaining agreement. These agreements tend to more clearly define such terms as professional day, immediate supervisor, instructional day, adjunct duties, and impasse.

Since the rules, regulations, and practices agreed to in the "contract" supercede district guidelines and practices, it is essential for every teacher to understand both the rights and responsibilities under these relatively new agreements. Whether you have, or have not, joined the local association, its negotiating team generally represents all full-time teachers at the bargaining table.

Responsibilities under the agreement will be enforced and violations noted by your immediate supervisor. This means that if you are required to be in your classroom at 7:45, you must be there at 7:45, not 7:50, or 8:00 a.m. If the "contract" calls for a statement of objectives to be filed by the teacher by October 1, it means October 1, not the 2nd, the 10th or later. If a staff member wants to transfer to another school, the procedure must be followed to the letter or the transfer request can be declared invalid. If the agreement says the teacher must call in by 7:00 a.m. in case of illness, calling after 7:00 a.m. could result in a loss of pay.

The point of all this for a new or experienced teacher is to be sure to read the contract, and to adhere strictly to the regulations. Ignorance of the terms of the agreement is not an acceptable excuse for any violations unwittingly committed. While these agreements do spell out carefully teacher responsibilities, they also (sometimes for the first time) detail teacher rights which previously may have been politely ignored. Such rights include protection of a teacher's personnel file, including proper access to the file and procedures for filing administrative memos. (Secret memos without the teacher's signature are generally not allowable). Rights regarding leaves of absence, sick leave, personal necessity leaves, bereavement leaves, and other types of leaves are also carefully spelled out. Even though these leaves were formerly included as board policies, they were usually open to interpretation by the personnel director or some other personnel officer. Agreements leave little room for interpretation and bring many of these matters into the open.

A good example of a relatively new development in teacher-district negotiations is the matter of teacher grievance rights. Formerly those matters were settled (usually in favor of management) at a local site. Most teacher units now make grievance procedures the heart of most agreements, taking up three, four, and five pages of explanation. Frequently, these procedures are couched in legalistic terms, sometimes binding, sometimes not.

How, then, should you use this newly-won right to better your teaching situation? It is not to your advantage to have the reputation of being a continual "rabble-rouser," "cry baby," or "guard-house lawyer." In other words, you would not want to grieve every minor situation. On the other hand, let's say that your supervisor (principal), on the strength of two ten-minute observations, makes a judgment that you should not be recommended for reemployment. Even though this is unlikely, it is possible. Your first step is not to get into an argument with the principal, but rather to consult the agreement and your teacher representative to check on proper evaluation procedures. Frequently, the matter can be settled at this level in a conversation with the principal. If the problem cannot be resolved, you then have recourse to invoke the grievance procedure. Usually, you will be required to file your grievance in writing within a specified number of days from the date of the alleged grievance.

Once you begin this procedure, you should have built a strong case based upon a definite violation of procedure. (Example: The agreement states that observations must last for a minimum of 15 to 20 minutes.) Your chances for success must be based upon *procedural violations,* not upon whether you think you are right and the principal wrong. To initiate a grievance based upon hearsay, hurt feelings, and emotionalism is foolhardy and leads to frustration and defeat.

In recapping this chapter, we have said that your classroom discipline problems can be better handled if you have a better grasp of options which are open to you. These options include a thorough knowledge of how to acquire a new position; how to prepare an effective resumé; how to interview effectively; and how to retain your current position by thoroughly understanding your rights and responsibilities. We maintain that this background will help you to achieve a peace of mind which will allow you to use your professional talents in the classroom more effectively.

How would you answer the following sample interview questions?

1. Are you a well organized person?

2. How do you discipline your students?

3. What are your major strengths and weaknesses?

4. How can a teacher tell when he or she has had a good class session? Give me an example please.

5. Can you recall when you first wanted to be a teacher?

6. Describe the characteristics of an effective teacher.

7. One of your students cheats on an examination. You see it. What would you do?

8. A teacher tells you, "Failure is good for students—it helps them to learn." How would you respond to this?

9. How do you feel when a student fails?

10. What books have you read lately?

11. What are your avocations?

12. Where do you expect to be in five years, professionally speaking?

13. What are your long- and short-range goals?

14. Do you enjoy sports as a participant? As an observer?

15. What is the role of a school principal in your opinion?

March 28, 1978

Mr. Newton H. Hart, Director of Personnel
Decatur Unified School District
315 E. Oak Street
Francine, Illinois 93277

Dear Mr. Hart:

    Please consider me a serious applicant for a position as
a learning disability teacher in the Decatur Unified School
District. Included with this letter of application is my
resumé as well as a list of current references. My placement
file is being forwarded to your office for your consideration.
    As my resumé indicates, I have had a variety of professional
experiences including special training in dealing with
emotionally disturbed children.
    I truly have a sincere interest in this position and will
await further word from you regarding a personal interview.

Sincerely,

Eugene F. Taylor

Enclosures (1)

August 1978

Name: Michael Gillis
Address: 2620 Associated Road, Springfield, Illinois 45672
Telephone: 592-5872
Date of Birth: February 9, 1949
Citizenship: United States
Marital Status: Married, 1 son

Areas of Teaching Competence

Regular classrooms in elementary school grades 1-6 (ages 6 to 10)
and middle school grades 8-10 (ages 12 to 16). Special education
in kindergarten-grade 12 (ages 5 to 18 years): with students
having learning disabilities, emotional problems or mental
retardation.

Educational Background:

Master of Education: Loyola College, Baltimore, Maryland
                        Course work completed Spring 1973, examination
                        taken August, 1973.
                        Degree in special education with emphasis on
                        teaching emotionally disturbed children.

Bachelor of Science: Pennsylvania State University, State College,
                        Pennsylvania, June, 1970.
                        Graduated with Distinction, having completed
                        major programs in elementary education and
                        special education (emphasis on mentally
                        retarded students).

Positions Held:

9/77 - 6/78   Educationally Handicapped Teacher; Hacienda-La Puente
                Unified School District, La Puente, California.
1/77 - 7/77   Remedial Teacher; Norwood Remedial School.
1/73 - 1/76   Remedial Teacher; Crossroads Center of Educational
                Therapy.
9/79 - 10/73   Special Education Teacher; Behavioral and Learning
                System Classroom, Bear Creek School, Baltimore
                County School System.
2/70 - 6/70   Student Teacher at Cresson State School for the
                Mentally Retarded; instructed students ages 7-23
                in a state institution.
9/69 - 12/69   Student Teacher at Central Bucks School District,
                Doyleston, Pennsylvania, normal second grade class.
6/68 - 9/68   Counselor for summer program at Devereux Foundation
                for the Emotionally Disturbed, West Chester,
                Pennsylvania.

Fellowships Held and Honors Received:

Two year university scholarship awarded by the Pennsylvania
Association for Retarded Children (9/68 - 6/70).
Graduated with Distinction from Pennsylvania State University,
June 1970.

Credentials:

Special Education K-12 - Maryland - Expiration 1980.
Educationally Handicapped K-12 - California - Authorizes service
teacher of mentally retarded, emotionally disturbed, and
educationally handicapped - Expiration 1982.

References:

Mr. Harry Bird	Principal of Fox Creek Elementary School, Del Haven and Melbourne Road, Dundalk, Maryland. Phone: 494-6822
Mrs. Betty Cates	Director of Special Education, Greenwood Center, Baltimore County Board of Education, Towson, Maryland. Phone: 494-7682
Roy B. Oates	Principal of Lassalette School, 14333 Lassalette Street, La Puente, California, 91744. Phone: 887-6942
Gene Grimes	Special Education Psychologist, Hacienda-La Puente Unified School District, Administrative Annex, 445 North Glendora Avenue, La Puente, California 91744. Phone: 574-2485

Placement File - #8369 University of Illinois

10 Solving the Puzzle: Effectively Joining Discipline and Instruction

The business of education is forming effective habits of discriminating tested beliefs from mere assertions, guesses, and opinions, to develop a lively, sincere and open-minded preference for conclusions that are properly grounded, and to ingrain into individuals' working habits methods of inquiry and reasoning appropriate to the various problems that present themselves.

John Dewey

Wherever you teach, whether it is in the inner city, in small towns amid peaceful farmlands, vast deserts or mountain ranges, in towns dominated by industry or other commercial enterprises, or in affluent suburbs, you will be faced with the same problems in tension, communication, instruction and goal achievement that all other teachers must face. Your students may look, speak, and dress differently than those 3000, 300, or even, 30 miles away, but they will also share the same problems. They will all need to learn about themselves, how to deal with others, and how to deal with school, home and societal pressures. Both teachers and students alike want to be successful and happy. No one enjoys failing. Everyone likes to be important and know they have self-worth. Thus, no matter what your stratum of society or geographical region, by the fact of your basic humanism you will share the same goals and pressures as all other teachers. But, how do you as an individual achieve these goals and deal with these pressures? This is what makes your teaching situation unique. Answering that question constitutes the teaching puzzle that we all must solve.

For the teacher, successfully solving this puzzle will mean that you can avoid or solve the day-by-day problems in your classroom that tend to chip away at your abilities, enthusiasm, and peace of mind. You will have prevented your students' potentially disruptive behavior and your classroom's environmental circumstances from impeding the effectiveness of your instructional program. Being in control of instruction and discipline, you will know how to channel student energies, will have assessed their needs and feelings, and will have effectively built a learning environment in which students work toward achieving their maximum potential, where you, parents, and staff members harmoniously work toward the accomplishment of both individual and group objectives.

How do you achieve this state of near perfection, you may well ask. The answer is simple. You achieve it only through considerable effort on your part, that of your students and that of everyone else who is directly and indirectly involved in the instructional program. No teacher walks into the classroom the first, 100th, or last day of the school year knowing all of the answers. And, unfortunately, there are no magic wands that turn instructional and disciplinary problems into star dust. You are the manager of the classroom work force and it is completely up to you to assign appropriate tasks and to motivate your student workers to willingly and effectively participate to the fullest while accomplishing those tasks. You must get them to learn as a group where no student disrupts group or individual learning or performance.

How is this reduction in disciplinary problems and construction of a cooperative and workable learning environment to be accomplished? Jesse Jackson believes that improved discipline will result from students, parents, and educators concentrating on the 5 A's of attendance, attention, atmosphere, attitude, and achievement. We mentioned in the preface that we thought it could be accomplished by the 3 C's of coping with student misbehavior, conquering school anxieties, and constructing vitally necessary positive programs of classroom discipline. Right now you could probably find fifteen other, equally viable, systems or philosophies described in journals and newsletters which call for various other letter groupings, teacher and school commitment and student, parent and community involvement all aimed at improving discipline and student learning.

As you listen to criticisms of the educational system today by both educators and non-educators alike, you hear increasingly calls for improving teaching and disciplinary practices, the weight of which rests heavily on the shoulders of teachers everywhere. Although you, as educators, are making strides, how do you improve the literacy levels of our students and educate more productive members of the ever-changing work force? Specifically, how do you motivate uninspired students to take part in learning activities that they, often rightfully, determine will have little value for them as adults when they will be faced with high unemployment or changing technology which result in dramatic changes in working conditions and needs? How do you emphasize the importance and value of education when PhD's are unable to find work in their chosen fields and engineers and teachers struggle to make ends meet or are unemployed and on welfare like many far less educated persons?

These frustrations and criticisms are additional obstacles to solving the teaching puzzle. However, if teachers and other curriculum managers have a clear understanding of these problems and concertedly work toward devising programs developed to provide appropriate educational experiences from kindergarten (and in many areas, pre-school) through high school, adult education and collegiate offering, they will meet both present individual needs as well as future individual and societal demands.

This curricular preparation, plus the knowledge you have of interpersonal dynamics, will provide the foundation for improving education both today and in the future. To be truly successful, teachers will need to be aware of the effects of many anthropological, biological, sociological, and psychological constructs upon the dealings of human beings which may be seen to be working in the classroom. One such understanding is that your students' assertion of rights, preferences, and biases may grow from their internal feelings that they have a territory to defend, whether it be their desk, a part of the playground or a hallway, or the entire school or neighborhood.[1] This knowledge may give you insight into their struggles with you and others.

We all occupy territories (both mental and physical) which we feel are our own, and will allow other people to enter only with permission and will fight to keep intruders out. Your major goal as a successful teacher will be to get invited into the students' mental territory while including them effectively in yours. The classroom territory cannot be one in which the strongest students suppress the weakest or disrupt the educational

---

[1] For further readings in this area: *The Territorial Imperative* by Robert Ardrey (New York: Dell Publishing Co.—a Delta book, 1966).

proceedings of all. It must be one in which territories are defined and maintained for both the teacher and students but one in which all may work together cooperatively to achieve both individual and group goals.

This goal achievement with the attendant understanding of individual needs and attitudes is accomplished, we believe, through the practice of anticipative action in the classroom. In this practice, we feel is developed a strategem, a mental teaching set, that pervades all activities, relationships and conflicts in the classroom. Whether you call it preventive teaching, anticipative action, or whatever, we are talking about the establishment of a habitual mode of thinking and acting which helps you to both avoid and deal more effectively with instructional and disciplinary problems.

Anticipative action is based upon the positive problem solving technique described in Chapter 6, Teacher Watch and Consult. From the time you enter that classroom before school starts at the beginning of the year (and possibly from the time you first interview for your teaching position), you constantly look for possible trouble-spots which may either lead to disruptive behavior or impede your instructional effectiveness and your students' learning. As you prepare to teach, as you arrange furniture, as you meet and deal with students, staff members and parents you must think ahead to what still may face you and decide how you can prevent problems. Each of our chapters has dealt with this process of pre-assessment, planning, instruction, and post-evaluation.

Anticipative action is used effectively in:

Relaxation of classroom tensions by identifying your own sources and signs of tension; and by attempting to control the effects of tension through the appropriate usage of self-fulfilling prophecies, avoidance of the fight-flight response, and improved and consistent problem solving practices.

Creating positive and productive school environments by analyzing the classroom and school physical environment to identify physical variables which might adversely affect student behavior and learning; and by structuring the environment to prevent or diminish troublesome disturbances.

Establishing effective student–teacher relationships by determining individual and group attitudes, goals and leadership patterns; and by using group dynamics to improve both individual and group functioning.

Improving curriculum while diminishing the effects of disruptive behaviors by discovering student needs for knowledge and skill development; and by designing a sequenced, realistic and flexible program which meets student needs and deals appropriately with curriculum based disturbances.

Coping with student misbehavior by observing classroom behavioral dynamics to determine exactly what and who is disruptive; and by preventing disruptions by consistent adherence to standards of appropriate behavior and effective employment of the Premack Principle of high probability/low probability behavior and contingency management.

Improving classroom communication by determining which verbal and nonverbal components of communication may adversely affect your communicative effectiveness, and by using the positive feedback of social and tangible reinforcers, assertive behavior and selective listening to improve communication while discouraging misbehavior.

Developing positive interpersonal relationships with school personnel and parents by knowing when and how to seek help with behavioral and/or instructional disturbances; and by dealing more effectively with student problems by contacting parent and school helpers before they are out of control and effectively gaining and giving support and information in parent–teacher conferences.

Successfully finding and retaining teaching positions by reducing tensions over job finding procedures, subsequent teaching evaluations and fulfillment of the teaching contract; and by maintaining up-to-date placement materials, and understanding your legal obligations and rights.

Throughout our entire discussion, the words discipline, instruction, and anxiety have been continuously linked. Your instructional program cannot be strong if your disciplinary program is weak. Neither program can be strong if you are overly tense and your tensions will be increased if your instruction and discipline are ineffective. Merging these three appropriately and successfully through the strategies outlined in anticipative action will ultimately result in your solving the teaching and disciplinary puzzle.

Ardrey, Robert, *The Territorial Imperative*. New York: Dell Publishing Co., Inc., 1966.

Dewey, John, *How We Think*. Lexington, Mass.: D. C. Heath & Company, 1901.

Jackson, Jesse, "Jesse Jackson: He Spells Discipline with Five A's," *Creative Discipline: Searching for the better way,* 1, No. 6–7, (April, June, 1978).

Index

A

Accomplishing the 3 C's, 208–209
Achievement tests, 182
Administrative attitudes
—and student discipline, 170
Ahlering, Inez
—student teacher reactions, 8, 17
Ancillary personnel
—and student group dynamics, 72
Anderson, Harold S.
—prospective teacher fears, 8, 17
Anticipative action
—and communication, 148
—and consistency, 31
—coping with student misbehavior, 211
—creating positive and productive school environments, 210
—curriculum structure, 84
—dealing with instructional and disciplinary problems, 210
—developing positive interpersonal relationships, 211
—direction giving, 93
—establishing effective student-teacher relationships, 210
—evaluative phase, 128
—flexibility in time management, 125
—improving classroom communication, 211
—improving curriculum while diminishing effects of disruptive behavior, 210
—instruction, 210
—instruction and discipline, 97
—interpersonal dynamics, 72
—merging behaviorism and humanism, 82
—planning, 210
—post-evaluation, 210
—pre-assessment, 210
—relaxation of classroom tensions, 210
—student discipline and seeking outside help, 171
—successful finding and retaining of teaching positions, 211

Anxiety
—beginning teachers, sources of, 8–9, 12
—collective bargaining, 190
—complexity of, 4–6
—definition, performance oriented, 7
—definitions, 6
—desensitization, 31
—discipline, 28
—effects of, 14–15
—experienced teachers, sources of, 10–12
—job finding, 211
—middle managers, 4–5
—personal, sources of, 4
—physiological modality, 28
—physiological signs, 24
—professional, sources of, 4
—recognizing, 24
—reducing, 24
—response modes (modalities), 6–7
—sensory relaxation, 31
—teacher evaluation, 190
—teacher expectations for the first day of school, 123
—transference, 15
Applicant responsibility, 195
Ardrey, Robert
—territoriality, 209, 212
Assertive behavior, 211
Assertive teaching, 159
—aggression vs. assertion, 161
—aim of, 160
—verbal and nonverbal elements of communication, 161
Assignment completion, 174

B

Baren, Martin
—childhood stress, 14, 15, 17
Baseline behavior, 127
Behavioral counters, 126
Behavioral managment, by students and teachers, 96
Behavioral problems
—determining the source, 128

214